Peer Teaching:
To Teach is To Learn Twice

By Neal A. Whitman

ASHE-ERIC Higher Education Report No. 4, 1988

Prepared by

Clearinghouse on Higher Education
The George Washington University

Published by

Association for the Study of
Higher Education

Jonathan D. Fife,
Series Editor

Cite as
Whitman, Neal A. *Peer Teaching: To Teach is To Learn Twice.*
ASHE-ERIC Higher Education Report No. 4. Washington, D.C.: Association for the Study of Higher Education, 1988.

Library of Congress Catalog Card Number 88-83592
ISSN 0884-0040
ISBN 0-913317-48–9

Managing Editor: Christopher Rigaux
Manuscript Editor: Katharine Bird
Cover design by Michael David Brown, Rockville, Maryland

The ERIC Clearinghouse on Higher Education invites individuals to submit proposals for writing monographs for the Higher Education Report series. Proposals must include:
1. A detailed manuscript proposal of not more than five pages.
2. A chapter-by-chapter outline.
3. A 75-word summary to be used by several review committees for the initial screening and rating of each proposal.
4. A vita.
5. A writing sample.

ERIC Clearinghouse on Higher Education
School of Education and Human Development
The George Washington University
One Dupont Circle, Suite 630
Washington, D.C. 20036-1183

ASHE Association for the Study of Higher Education
Texas A&M University
Department of Educational Administration
Harrington Education Center
College Station, Texas 77843

This publication was prepared partially with funding from the Office of Educational Research and Improvement, U.S. Department of Education, under contract no. ED RI-88-062014. The opinions expressed in this report do not necessarily reflect the positions or policies of OERI or the Department.

EXECUTIVE SUMMARY

The purpose of this report is to describe efforts in higher education to use students as teachers, thereby providing them with the benefits traditionally enjoyed by their professors. Certainly, peer teaching is not a new concept. From the ancient Greek use of student leaders as *archons* to the nineteenth century English and American use of older students to drill younger students in classrooms, educators have found that the students who do the teaching benefit from their own learning gains (Wagner 1982).

What Is Peer Teaching and What Is the Psychological Basis for its Benefits?

The first published reports of students teaching students in situations planned and directed by their professors began to appear in the 1960s (Goldschmid and Goldschmid 1976). An impetus for these peer teaching programs was dissatisfaction of faculty with large lecture courses in which students played a passive role. By using undergraduate students as teaching assistants and tutors, peer teachers and peer learners were able to play a more active role in the learning process.

Peer teachers benefit because in reviewing and organizing the material to be taught, student teachers gain a better understanding of the subject. Studies demonstrate that the cognitive processing used to study material to teach is different from studying to take a test (Bargh and Schul 1980, Benware and Deci 1984), and the peer learners benefit because of the ability of peers to teach at the right level (Schwenk and Whitman 1984). In general, both parties seem to benefit from the cooperative relationship that peer teaching generates (Whipple 1987).

What Types of Peer Teaching Are Used in Higher Education?

There are five types of peer teaching used in higher education. In three types, the peer teacher is more advanced than the learner. These are "near-peers," and include undergraduate teaching assistants, tutors, and counselors. *Undergraduate teaching assistants* usually are students who recently were successful in the course, and they are useful because they provide a means to supplement large lecture courses with small discussion groups. *Tutors* also are previously successful students, but they teach on a one-to-one basis students who need extra help.

Counselors are similar to tutors in that they teach on a one-to-one basis. But, unlike teaching assistants and tutors affiliated with a specific course, counselors usually have a more general focus. They can provide help with course selection, study habits, and writing skills. The Writing Center at Brooklyn College is considered a model program in which students help students improve their writing skills (Bruffee 1978).

In the other two types of peer teaching, partnerships and work group, students are "co-peers" in that they are at the same level. *Partnerships* refer to one-to-one relationships in which two students interact as teacher and learner, and *work groups* refer to student groups sharing a common task.

What Strategies Should Academic Planners Consider?

When considering the implementation of peer teaching programs, academic planners should consider whether there will be resistance to change. Faculty may feel that students are replacing "real" teachers, so two-way communication is needed. Also, a public relations campaign may be important so that a positive image is presented to faculty and students. From the start, planners should consider meeting with faculty and student groups, putting the goals and objectives in writing, and offering orientation and training to student recruits. In addition, providing evaluation results may be helpful in winning and maintaining the support of administrators (Starks 1984).

Faculty involvement in the recruitment, selection, and training of peer teachers is a key to program success (Walker, Von Bargen, and Wessner 1980). As an adjunct to training, providing manuals to guide peer teachers can be a helpful resource (deSilva and Freund 1985). Basically, what is required for successful implementation is a systematic approach (Williams 1981).

What Can the Classroom Teacher Do to Implement Peer Teaching?

Aside from campus-wide efforts to plan and conduct peer teaching programs, individual college classroom teachers can use peer teaching to increase student involvement. One technique, known as "creative dialogue," requires that the teacher write discussion questions on the blackboard and organize students into small discussion groups (Tighe 1971). Other techniques were described in *Change* magazine's *Guide to Effective Teachers* (Meeth 1978). For example, upperclass teaching assistants can lead discussion groups, writing tutors can give feedback to students, and foreign language students can form conversation groups.

In using students as teachers, faculty may find that a strong motivation for peer teachers is the added contact with faculty. Many students enjoy the opportunity to plan and conduct programs with their professors and to feel as if they are colleagues. In fact, peer teaching can be a means to recruit future college teachers.

The Need for Additional Research
A problem with existing evaluation studies is that there rarely is a control group of students in a traditional approach using the same learning materials. Also, evaluation of peer teaching programs is hampered by fluid changes in the programs: They do not stand still long enough to be measured (Giddan and Austin 1982). Given the lack of resources, it is understandable that in-depth evaluation may be lacking.

Thus, much available evidence regarding peer teaching is in the form of anecdotes and impressions. Questions which researchers should consider include: What is the best type of training for peer teachers? What types of students will benefit most from peer teaching? What is the role of the college professor in peer teaching programs? A basic research question is, How do students learn to learn collaboratively?

Notwithstanding the need for additional research, it seems clear that student peer groups are such a potent force, with or without faculty direction, that faculty should consider channeling this force in positive ways. Providing opportunities for students to teach each other may be one of the most important services a teacher can render.

Conclusions

- Although, traditionally, students are expected to do their own work, learning also may occur when students work cooperatively.
- Both peer teachers and learners learn.
- Involving students in the planning of peer teaching programs helps to develop future college teachers.
- Students like to become peer teachers because they seek closer relationships with faculty.
- Learning may increase with a blend of situations in which professors are present and are not present.

ADVISORY BOARD

Zelda F. Gamson
Director
New England Resource Center for Higher Education

J. Wade Gilley
Senior Vice President
George Mason University

Judy Diane Grace
Director of Research
Council for Advancement and Support of Education

Madeleine F. Green
Director, Center for Leadership Development
American Council on Education

Milton Greenberg
Provost
American University

Judith Dozier Hackman
Associate Dean
Yale University

Paul W. Hartman
Vice Chancellor for University Relations and Development
Texas Christian University

James C. Hearn
Associate Professor
University of Minnesota

Evelyn Hively
Vice President for Academic Programs
American Association of State Colleges and Universities

Frederic Jacobs
Dean of the Faculties
American University

Paul Jedamus
Professor
University of Colorado

George Keller
Senior Vice President
The Barton-Gillet Company

Oscar T. Lenning
Vice President for Academic Affairs
Robert Wesleyan College

Charles J. McClain
President
Northeast Missouri State University

Judith B. McLaughlin
Research Associate on Education and Sociology
Harvard University

Marcia Mentkowski
Direector of Research and Evaluation
Professor of Psychology
Alverno College

Richard I. Miller
Professor, Higher Education
Ohio University

James L. Morrison
Professor
University of North Carolina

Elizabeth M. Nuss
Executive Director
National Association of Student Personnel Administrators

Robert L. Payton
Director, Center on Philanthropy
Indiana University

Karen T. Romer
Associate Dean for Academic Affairs
Brown University

Jack E. Rossmann
Professor of Psychology
Macalester College

Donald M. Sacken
Associate Professor
University of Arizona

Robert A. Scott
President
Ramapo College of New Jersey

William R. Whipple
Director, Honors Programs
University of Maine

CONTENTS

FOREWORD

On the surface, there appears to be a number of reasons why peer teaching is attractive. Clearly, it is an inexpensive way to hold small classes with fewer students. It also increases both general productivity and small group student interactions. There are, however, three other major reasons why peer teaching has major appeal.

First, peer teaching enhances the college socialization process as described in Ann Bragg's *Socialization Process in Higher Education* (Report 7, 1976). As Bragg reports, one of the major lasting contributions made by a college education is the reinforcement and development of specific behavior patterns and intellectual values. Small group classes, led by a peer teacher, greatly contribute to that socialization process. The peer teacher serves as a "significant other" or role model that has proven to be even more effective in many cases than traditional teachers in instilling enthusiasm towards learning.

The second major reason is, as indicated by the subtitle of this report, that "to teach is to learn twice". Individuals who experience a course as a student and then return to the same course as a peer teacher develop an understanding of the material from two very different perspectives. This intellectual return to the peer teacher may make the experience one of the most intellectually rewarding of a student's career.

A third reason that should be a major consideration for higher education in general is that the experience of peer teaching may instill a desire in the peer teachers to pursue their education and a career in college teaching. It is fairly well accepted that, all things remaining equal, there will be a significant shortage of qualified faculty in the mid-1990s. Anything an institution can do to promote the renewal of the professoriate will help ensure its long-term intellectual viability.

There are of course other considerations, positive and negative, concerning peer teaching. This report, the fourth written for the series by Neal Whitman of the University of Utah's Medical Center, examines many aspects of the peer teaching process. He offers both planning strategies for administrators and specific classroom techniques for faculty.

Given higher education's pressing need to instill in all its students a renewed respect for teaching ability, any report offering a way of doing just that should be given the most careful consideration at all levels.

Jonathan D. Fife
Professor and Director
ERIC Clearinghouse on Higher Education
School of Education and Human Development
The George Washington University

ACKNOWLEDGMENTS

The author would like to thank Elaine Weiss, President of Educational Dimensions, for her assistance and counsel. Her modeling of one of this report's themes, collaborative learning, is recognized widely and appreciated.

PEER TEACHING AND THE PSYCHOLOGICAL BASIS FOR ITS BENEFITS

The purpose of this report is to describe efforts in higher education to use students as teachers, thereby providing them with the benefits traditionally enjoyed by their professors: the opportunity to learn by teaching. Most teachers know that the best way to learn is to teach (Martin 1981). In a similar vein, the Mathematical Society of America recently quoted the early nineteenth century French philosopher, Joseph Joubert, "To teach is to learn twice" (Raimi 1981). Because "learning twice" may sound repetitive, the reader may wonder if "learning more deeply" better describes the benefit of teaching others. In any case, what is recommended in this report is that faculty should take advantage of the mutual benefits that accrue when students teach each other. Proponents of this strategy first appeared in elementary and secondary schools. Early supporters of peer-mediated instruction noted, "It has long been obvious that children learn from their peers, but a more significant observation is that *children learn more from teaching other children*" (Gartner, Kohler, and Riessman 1971, p. 1). Faculty whose field is elementary education may wish to consult Ehly and Eliason's 1980 bibliography of peer teaching which includes over 500 references.

Faculty should take advantage of the mutual benefits that accrue when students teach each other.

Faculty whose field is English composition may wish to consult two historical treatments of student writing groups, Gere (1987) and Holt (1988). Gere traces classroom writing groups to literary societies in American colleges between the colonial period and the middle of the nineteenth century and considers the influence of late nineteenth century curriculum reform movements on contemporary writing group advocates. Gere's chronological listing of books and articles about writing groups is particularly helpful because of her annotations. Holt's sociohistorical treatment of writing groups in her doctoral dissertation also is well-documented, with her analysis based on the examination of articles in academic journals from 1911 to 1986. Both authors observe that, although peer teaching has a rich tradition, peer teaching programs often are described as innovative or new.

Certainly, peer teaching is not a new concept. In an excellent historical perspective, Wagner traces peer teaching back to Aristotle's use of *archons* or student leaders. "Peer teaching has alternatively lapsed into obscurity or seen a resurgence of effort" since the first century A.D. (Wagner, 1982, p. 3). For example, in the early nineteenth century, Joseph Lancaster's "monitoring system," in which students drilled each other, was popular in England and the United States. In her review of the literature, Wagner found scant mention of peer teaching from the latter part of the nineteenth century until the 1960s. Then, numerous educators began to refer to the use of peer teachers in the one-room schools of rural America in the late nineteenth and early twentieth centuries. For example:

> *Teachers in one-room rural schools often called upon their older students to help teach the younger ones. They did so in the hope that younger children would benefit from the extra attention and help they got from their tutors and that the older children, proud to be cast as assistant teachers, would be motivated to improve their own school work* (Lippitt and Lippitt 1968, p. 24).

Another historical perspective also identified the one-room classroom as an important root in the peer teaching movement:

> *The first image that comes to mind when one thinks of children teaching other children is that of little red schoolhouses that were staffed by one dedicated teacher. As a result of having a variety of students to instruct, these teachers frequently relied upon the older or more intelligent students to work with the other children* (Ehly and Larsen 1980, p. 10).

According to Ehly and Larsen's review of the literature, peer teaching programs for children of the same grade seldom are mentioned; most frequently mentioned are studies of cross-age tutoring, for instance, older students teaching younger students. One might consider graduate students who are teaching assistants for undergraduate students to be a current form of cross-age peer teaching in higher education. However, in this volume they will not be viewed in this light. The author's view is that graduate assistants are more akin to junior faculty than to college student peers. However, upperclassmen teaching underclassmen will be included as examples of peer teaching.

"As any college student can attest, paid tutors can be found on every campus in the country, or at least in every college town" (Ehly and Larsen 1980, p. 228). However, for the purposes of this report, *peer teaching will refer to students teaching students in situations that are planned and directed by a teacher*. In peer teaching, students learn through doing tasks organized by teachers, but brought about through a variety of situations and tasks in which students work together.

One of the first teachers to plan and direct peer teaching in higher education was Marcel Goldschmid at McGill University, Montreal. He reported that the impetus for experimenting with instructional options was his dissatisfaction with the lecture method in large undergraduate classes of 200 to 300 students. He thought that lecturing as a routine teaching method was ineffective because it forced the college student to be passive, and provided little or no exchange between the professor and the students and the students themselves. Goldschmid decided to offer students four instructional options. In the *discussion group option*, six to 12 students met twice a week for one hour, choosing a topic and specific reading assignments before each meeting. In the *seminar group option*, three to four students individually prepared five-minute papers which they presented to the group of 10 to 12 students in each of the two weekly meetings. Each presentation was followed by a group discussion (Goldschmid 1970).

The third was the *learning cell option* pioneered by a mathematics lecturer at McGill, Donald Kingsbury. In this option, pairs of students meet for one hour and change partners at each session twice a week. The students take turns quizzing each other and discussing the reading material. In the *fourth option*, students individually prepare a long essay, meeting in groups four times during the course to discuss their outlines and progress. Goldschmid (1970) offered the four options in a psychology course, and based on postcourse student surveys, found that an overwhelming number of students wished that these options were available in all their courses.

The first published literature review of college peer teaching showed that experimentally-controlled efforts were not widespread in North America until the 1960s (Goldschmid and Goldschmid 1976). However, since the 1950s, college educators had recognized that peer influence among students is a powerful, but wasted, resource (Newcomb 1962). Tyler (1975) stated in the 1970s that the failure to use peer teaching in various forms was a major source of waste in U.S. schools. The potential contribution of peer teachers to higher education was discussed by Wrigley. He thought that there was an inconsistency between what was taught and what was practiced in undergraduate psychology courses: Students are taught that active learning is more effective than passive, yet "we do not follow our own counsel when we teach" (1973, p. 5). The challenge is to find active forms of learning which do not cost too much. His solution was to devise ways for undergraduates to teach one another: "Our great reservoir of idle and cheap talent is clearly the undergraduates themselves" (Wrigley 1973, p. 5).

Because the student peer group is such a potent force in student development, Mayhew and Ford (1971) suggested that the curriculum be reorganized to make maximum use of peer groups. They reported, for example, that Florida State University used block scheduling of the same students into the same courses to encourage student interaction and found greater across-the-board achievement. Also, they reported dramatic gains at Boston University where students not eligible for a bachelor's degree program as freshmen were organized into peer support groups for two years.

Before (1) identifying the types of peer teaching that are being used in higher education, (2) describing strategies for implementation, (3) recommending techniques for college teachers who wish to incorporate peer teaching in their courses, and (4) suggesting future research needs, it will help to explain the psychological basis for peer teaching effectiveness. Peer teaching can be considered a subset of the collaborative learning movement in higher education. The steering committee of the American Association of Higher Education's Action Community on Collaborative Learning stated:

> Collaborative learning in undergraduate education is a pedagogical style that emphasizes cooperative efforts among students, faculty, and administrators.... it benefits participants by making them more active as learners and more interactive as teachers (Whipple 1987, p. 3).

The observation that the peer teacher or tutor benefits is not new. The Moravian teacher, John Comenius, wrote in 1632,

> The saying, "He who teaches others, teaches himself," is very true, not only because constant repetition impresses a fact indelibly on the mind, but because the process of teaching in itself gives a deeper insight into the subject taught (Gartner, Kohler, and Riessman 1971, pp. 14–15).

"Constant repetition" and "deeper insight" are reasons on a cognitive level that explain why learning through teaching works. There are reasons on an affective level, as well. Both the *cognitive* and *affective* levels will be discussed here.

Cognitive Level

Gartner, Kohler, and Riessman (1971) summarized a number of beneficial cognitive processes that occur in preparation for teaching. (1) *The teacher must review the material.* Even if already known, this review may help the teacher grasp it more fully or deeply. (2) *The teacher must organize the material to be presented.* This process may lead the teacher to seek out examples and illustrations to help explain the material. Moreover, the teacher may reorganize the facts in a new way, leading to a reformulation of the subject. (3) *To teach the subject, the teacher may need to seek out its basic structure and, in so doing, may gain a better understanding of it.* These cognitive processes may have been the same that led the Nobel prizewinning physicist, Ernest Rutherford (1871–1937), to believe that he had not completed a scientific discovery until he was able to explain it to others (Highet 1950). A problem with higher education, as Wagner sees it, is that traditional course requirements ask students to demonstrate that they can present information to those who already have it, their teachers. Instead, the real test of academic excellence is communicating clearly about matters unknown to others, for example, to fellow students (Wagner 1987).

When people learn material for their own needs, is their cognitive processing different than when they learn for the purpose of teaching others? Bargh and Schul (1980) found that students in a teaching situation scored higher on an achievement test than those who did not teach. They suggested that preparing to teach someone else could produce a more highly organized cognitive structure. They concluded that this can occur both prior to and during instruction; someone preparing to teach will reorganize the material for clearer presentation and while actively teaching may reorganize or clarify material on the spot.

Benware and Deci (1984) hypothesized that the psychological processes involved in learning material to teach it may be different than those required to learn it. To test this hypothesis, they randomly assigned students in a university introductory psychology course to two groups: 21 in the experimental group and 22 in the control group. Both groups were asked to read and study an article on brain functioning. The *experimental group* was told that they would teach the contents of the article

to another student. The *control group* was told that they would be tested on the material. When students returned two weeks later, both groups were examined. The *experimental* group never taught the material.

The dependent variable to assess learning was a 24–item examination: 50 percent of the point value was assigned to rote memory and 50 percent to conceptual understanding. There was not a significant difference in rote memory, but the experimental group's higher scores for conceptual understanding were significant statistically. The explanation for this was that the prospect of teaching material facilitates intrinsic motivation for learning in students. The result is more active mental engagement compared to learning aimed simply at passing an examination (Benware and Deci 1984).

In addition to cognitive benefits in the preparation stage, there may be additional benefits that occur during the process of teaching. Reorganizing and clarifying material on the spot already has been mentioned. A review of research studies of groups learning educational material that systematically measured interactions in groups found a positive relationship in four out of five studies between giving help in groups and achievement (Webb 1982). The research finding suggested that explaining to others may be more beneficial to the explainer when the material is complex, requiring integration or reorganization, than when the material is simple or straightforward. It should be noted that none of the studies reviewed by Webb involved college-level students, and all the studies involved groups studying mathematics. The applicability of these results to higher education and to other subject areas could be questioned, although the conclusion (explaining complex material may lead to higher achievement for the explainer) has face validity.

In a study which involved college students (130 female college students in a history course in a midwestern university), those who prepared to teach and taught the contents of a 1,525-word article tested higher than those who only prepared to teach. Both groups tested higher than those who were taught and those who taught themselves (Annis 1983). Annis concluded that a possible explanation for these results lies in a three-stage theory of learning that involves (1) paying attention to material to be learned, (2) coding it in a personally meaningful way, and (3) associating it with what is already known. Students who prepared to teach and taught may have learned the most because their responsibilities required them to perform all three of the steps essential to learning.

A cognitive mechanism to account for learning that results from explaining material is the mere act of *verbalizing*. Durling and Schick (1976) studied learning in subjects who discussed material with a peer, with a confederate supposedly learning the task, and with the experimenter who already had mastered the task. Students talking with a peer or confederate performed significantly better than students speaking with the experimenter. Durling and Schick concluded that verbalizing for the purpose of helping another person understand material produces benefits not gained from verbalizing to demonstrate self-mastery of the material.

Affective Level

In a review of college counseling programs, Whitman, Spendlove, and Clark (1984) found that not only did college students make excellent peer counselors, but that the act of peer counseling was an effective strategy for self-help. In other words, college students can "help themselves by helping other students" (p. 28). This notion, formulated by Riessman (1965) as the *"helper therapy principle,"* was applied successfully in the health care system by Alcoholics Anonymous, and many other groups of patients with chronic problems. In these groups, it is clear that people giving help are profiting from their role as helper:

> *An age-old therapeutic approach is the use of people with a problem to help other people who have the same problem in a more severe form. But in the use of this approach... it may be that emphasis is being placed on the wrong person in centering attention on the person receiving help. More attention might well be given the individual who needs help less, that is, the person who is providing the assistance, because frequently it is he who improves* (Riessman 1965, p. 27).

In applying the *"helper therapy principle"* to students, Riessman noted that some children, when removed from a class in which they are below average and placed in a new group in which they are in the upper half of the class, stand out more as more is expected of them. He postulated that students at all levels may benefit from being in a situation where they can help others. In other words, some students develop intellectually and emotionally by being put into the tutor-helper role: "As any teacher can report, there is nothing like learning through teaching. By having to explain something to someone else, one's attention is focused more sharply" (Riessman 1965, p. 30). In analyzing the benefits to the peer teacher, Gartner, Kohler, and Riessman (1971) acknowledged that the relationship between self-confidence on the part of the peer teacher and learning was complicated, but seems to help explain on an emotional level why peer teachers benefit.

In a study of college student volunteers working with mentally ill patients, Holzberg, Knapp, and Turner (1966) found that increased personal competence led to results which showed more self-acceptance and awareness and tolerance of others. Related benefits to peer teachers were identified by Pierce, Stahlbrand, and Armstrong (1984), who observed that the most salient characteristic of the role of teacher is helping another person. Instead of being recipients of help, the traditional student role, "a positive consequence of placing students in the teacher role is that they derive the psychological dividends of helping another person" (p. 3).

In their review of peer teaching in higher education, Goldschmid and Goldschmid (1976) observed that peer teaching increased tutors' motivation to learn and self-esteem. However, measurement of these *affective* benefits of peer teaching is more difficult than measurement of *cognitive* benefits. In a study of college students in a psychology course who studied an article to either teach the contents or take a test, Benware and Deci (1984) made an effort to measure *affective* benefits of peer teaching by at least asking students for perceived effects. The students who studied the material to teach it reported more interest in the content than students who studied the material to be tested. Also, students who studied to teach reported that they perceived themselves more actively involved as learners when studying to teach versus studying to be tested. However, the control group, perhaps because they never had the experience of studying to teach, did not report the two types of learning as differentially active.

Peer Learning
Research shows that student "teachers" and "learners" benefit from peer teaching both *cognitively* and *affectively*, especially if they have the opportunity to alternate between roles. "One

could easily imagine a campus where all students are learners *and* teachers at different times and in different subjects, thus facilitating social interactions and enhancing learning'' (Goldschmid 1976, p. 441).

Of course, peer teaching would not be feasible if there were no peer learning. While it is difficult to make quantitative estimates of the effects of any teachers on student achievement (Mood 1970), peer teachers are believed to benefit learners because of (1) *their closeness as peers*, and (2) *the individualization that occurs when peer teaching is conducted as a one-to-one relationship* (Gartner, Kohler, and Riessman 1971). In higher education, Goldschmid and Goldschmid (1976) emphasized the sociopsychological benefits to learners of close personal contact in an otherwise remote environment.

The ability of peer teachers to effectively transmit material to learners was highlighted by Schwenk and Whitman (1984) in a handbook on teaching skills for medical residents. They pointed out that medical school faculty, who are ''unconsciously competent,'' may have difficulty teaching a medical procedure to residents. However, other residents who just have learned the procedure may find it easier to teach because they are ''consciously competent,'' that is, they still have to think through each step of the procedure, one step at a time.

In response to the question, ''What do you teach?'', a professor could answer ''college English'' or ''college students.'' The former implies a relationship between teacher and subject, the latter between teacher and students. Peer teaching emphasizes a relationship between learners. These relationships are explored in two essays by Bruffee (1984 and 1986) which are important because they have provided a dialogue in the peer teaching movement. In the 1984 essay, he argues that all humans are involved in a continuous conversation. Educational programs are most effective when students actively participate in this conversation and learn to talk reflectively with each other.

In the 1986 essay, Bruffee observes that the language used by most scholars to discuss and write about university instruction is *cognitive* in derivation.

The human mind is equipped with two working elements, a mirror and an inner eye. The mirror reflects outer reality. The inner eye contemplates that reflection. Reflection and contemplation together are what, from this cognitive point of view, we typically call thought or knowledge (Bruffee 1986, p. 776).

This *cognitive* view assumes that there is a universal structure behind knowledge and that new ideas are the products of individual minds. Bruffee takes a *social constructionist* view that assumes there is no universal structure behind knowledge; rather, there is a temporary consensus arrived at by communities of knowledgeable peers. It credits the community—not its individual members—for generating new ideas.

In her analysis of the social construction of knowledge, Andersen (1987) suggests that historically women have been excluded from its creation. She concludes that not only should women be included in the process, but that women's ways of knowing, which may differ from men's, should be included. Building on this notion, faculty interested in peer teaching may wish to mobilize cross-sex peer teaching as a means to expand the horizons of both men and women.

In seeking more community in the world of intellect, Palmer (1987) thinks that there are promising directions in the emergence of new epistemologies, for example, in women's, black, and native American studies. He argues these ways of knowing provide other ways of seeing and being in the world.

The *social construction* model relates to peer teaching because it assumes that learning occurs among persons rather than between a person and things. When students collaborate with other students and teachers, they join the community of knowledgeable peers, generating and testing new ideas and participating in the consensus over what is regarded as reality. For example, Abercrombie's experience was that medical students became better diagnosticians when they trained in groups because, when student views differed, the struggle toward concensus resulted in uncovering biases in judgment (Bruffee 1978). This notion of students as participants in scholarship mirrors the principle of adult education, *"Adults who actively seek to enhance proficiencies tend to see themselves as users of, rather then recipients of, education"* (Knox 1980, p. 79).

The notion that student collaboration and cooperation makes good practice was highlighted in a study supported by the American Association of Higher Education, the Education Commission of the States, and the Johnson Foundation:

Learning is enhanced when it is more like a team effort than a solo race. Good learning, like good work, is collaborative and social, not competitive and isolated. Working with others often increases involvement in learning. Sharing one's own ideas and responding to others' reactions improves thinking and deepens understanding (Chickering and Gamson 1987, p. 4).

Astin (1987) suggests that current teaching techniques do not encourage cooperation and that the existing curriculum does not give students the opportunity to learn effective leadership and teamwork skills. He recommends that faculty examine how they teach their classes and treat their students. An aim of this higher education report is to describe one way to teach classes and treat students differently—mobilize students as peer teachers.

Collaborative learning and peer teaching raise profound philosophical questions about the nature of authority. They point toward the issue of whether (1) knowledge is something which must be delivered from authorities, or whether (2) it is something which can be generated in the dialogue which takes place among those who seek to learn. A more extensive philosophical analysis of these philosophical questions would be welcome, but such a discussion would go beyond the scope of this report.

Summary

This higher education report reviews the efforts of students in undergraduate, graduate, and professional school programs to teach fellow students. Peer teaching is a type of collaborative learning with which both "teacher" and "learner" benefit. In seeking to describe the psychological basis for the benefits of peer teaching, no general theory to account for observable benefits has been presented, and the reader may feel disappointed that the question is not fully answered. No general theory has been presented because the research is scant and diffuse, and it would be premature to attempt to coalesce these findings into a systematic theory. More research to describe the benefits of peer teaching and to explain their psychological basis would be welcome.

TYPES OF PEER TEACHING USED IN HIGHER EDUCATION

After a decade of peer teaching efforts in higher education, Goldschmid and Goldschmid (1976) published their first review. They identified *five types* of peer teaching.

1. *Discussion groups* led by student teaching assistants are used to supplement large lectures. In some cases, students who previously have done well in the course are asked to help prepare and correct exams as well as to lead group discussions.
2. As an element of the Personalized System of Instruction (PSI) developed by Keller, students act as *proctors* who work on a one-to-one basis with students taking the course. The proctor's role is to administer tests on the numerous course units worked through by the individual students and give constructive feedback on the test results. Proctors also may let the course director know how their students are doing and report any problems with course material.
3. Course directors organize students into *work groups* conducted by the students themselves. The purpose of student groups is to increase participation. In some cases, the groups may work completely independently of the teacher, or may periodically report to the teacher.
4. Students are organized into *learning cells* in which two or three students alternately ask and answer questions on commonly read material, or critique each other's written work.
5. *Student counseling* occurs outside the classroom when students seek assistance at a counseling center where trained students are available to provide one-to-one help. The student counselor may review study habits, recommend strategies for improving a grade, or provide feedback on course assignments before work is turned in to the teacher.

Goldschmid and Goldschmid's review is a seminal work and should be consulted for an overview of peer teaching efforts made up to 1975.

Goldschmid and Goldschmid's review is a seminal work and should be consulted for an overview of peer teaching efforts made up to 1975. They describe important factors which contributed to the interest in peer teaching in higher education and discuss some of the issues and problems presented by this educational strategy. Building upon their model, five types of peer teaching will be described according to the organization shown on table 1. In three types, the peer teacher is more advanced

Table 1

PEER TEACHING MODELS
NEAR-PEERS:
1. Teaching Assistants
2. Tutors
3. Counselors
CO-PEERS:
4. Partnerships
5. Work Groups

than the learner. These peer teachers are called *"near-peers"* in this typology and include *undergraduate teaching assistants, tutors,* and *counselors.* In types four and five, the peer teacher is a co-student. These *"co-peers"* include *partnerships* and *working groups.* Of course, since the word "peer" by definition refers to equality of status, the use of "co-peer" may seem unnecessary. The term "co-peer" is used only to emphasize the collegial status of students who teach each other versus "near-peers" who teach fellow students. Nevertheless, what is common to "co-peer" and "near-peer" teaching is the power of tapping the resources of peer-group influence.

Teaching Assistants
It is a common practice for graduate students to be used as teaching assistants in undergraduate courses. Teaching assistants are useful because they provide an affordable means to supplement large lecture courses with weekly discussion groups, and, presumably, graduate students benefit from the teaching experience, particularly if they are headed for an academic career. For the purpose of this higher education report, graduate students teaching undergraduate students will not be considered a form of peer teaching. However, occasionally undergraduates are recruited to serve as teaching assistants. In these cases, we will consider the teaching assistants to be *"near-peers,"* in the sense that these peer teachers may be more advanced than their students, but not so far advanced to no longer be considered peers.

Churchill and John (1958) reported an early effort to use undergraduates as teaching assistants. The stated motivation was to save the teacher's time. They compared test results for mathematics students at Antioch College who were taught in small lecture-discussion sessions (20 to 30 students each) with a laboratory led by the instructor to those taught in a large lecture (70 students) with discussion sessions and laboratories led by an upperclass student assistant. Based on pre- and posttests, the two types of classes did not differ in the amount of knowledge gained and both groups gained significantly. Since the instructor's time commitment in the instructor-only format was 18 hours a week and in the instructor-upperclass student format was only four hours a week, the investigators concluded that using an undergraduate teaching assistant could save significant time for a college teacher without negatively affecting student learning.

However, Churchill and John (1958) acknowledged that, on a postcourse survey, students rated the instructor's presentation in the small lecture-discussion sections more favorably compared to the large lectures, and rated the instructor-led laboratories over the student-led ones more favorably. While suggesting that the shortcomings of large lecture presentations may be overcome with small laboratory sections, they did not address the expressed preference by students for both components of the instructor-only methodology. Because this study was conducted in 1956–57, the reader may be tempted to draw conclusions about faculty attitudes toward student preferences in the prestudent revolution of the 1960s.

Certainly, reports of using undergraduate teaching assistants since the 1960s have emphasized benefits to the students enrolled in the courses and to the teaching assistants rather than time savings for the college teachers. Of course, perhaps saving time remains a motive, albeit unstated. As an example of the prostudent use of undergraduate teaching assistants, Maas and Pressler (1973) described a program at Cornell University for six years in which students who had received an A in a large introductory psychology course were given academic credit the first time and a stipend the second time they served as teaching assistants. Students and faculty rated the undergraduate teaching assistants as high or higher than graduate teaching assistants, and results of questionnaires indicated that the student teachers believed they had benefited greatly from the experience, both intellectually and emotionally.

Based on informal interviews, Romer (1988) reported widespread praise at Brown University for the contributions made by undergraduate teaching assistants: "Praise from faculty who use them and praise from those students who have been helped by them" (p. 8). An expressed advantage undergraduates had over graduate students as teaching assistants was that they had taken the course in which they are TAs only a year or two before. Thus, based on their own personal experience, they can identify problems students may be having with the course material.

In addition to getting a chance to work with faculty and getting to know them better, undergraduate TAs reported a number of motivators more important than the pay, which generally is low:

Students cite the experience as exciting and interesting. They see it as an opportunity to learn the material more richly, more fully; to think about it, help others learn, discover new aspects of it one hadn't really understood that well before (Romer 1988, p. 8).

An undergraduate teaching assistant effort at Brown University is the Science Mentor Program, aimed at helping nonscience majors in science courses. Participating students attend an extra weekly session led by a "science mentor," an undergraduate science major. According to the faculty director, participants belong to three overlapping categories: "those who were apprehensive about science, those with limited background in science, and those who wished to reflect on science and its applications in a small-group situation" (Heywood 1988, p. 213). Based on student comments, Heywood concluded that the program was helpful. Students said that the science mentors helped make the course material more interesting and more understandable. A representative student commented:

The science mentor taught us how to study. Not only were we supposed to read and study the text and lecture notes, but reproduce diagrams as well. I took Biomed 5 last semester and I nearly failed the course because I did not know how to study. Now in Biomed 6 I just found out that I received a 90 on the exam. I never thought I could do it! Thank you (Heywood 1987, p. 213).

Tutors
Whereas teaching assistants are near-peers who teach small groups, tutors teach on a one-to-one basis. Undergraduate tu-

tors, called "proctors," comprise a key element of PSI (Personalized System of Instruction) pioneered by Keller. The salient feature of PSI is self-pacing of students through each unit of a course (Keller 1974). Mastery of each unit is required by testing, and proctors work individually with students, helping them with the material, administering tests, and giving feedback. Although PSI started with the teaching of psychology, Keller reported a sampling of over 400 courses using PSI, including the fields of biology, chemistry, English, engineering, mathematics, physics, sociology, and statistics.

Peer tutors are not confined to PSI courses. For example, Riley and Huffman (1980) described a peer support program at the University of North Carolina at Charlotte in which senior education majors participating in a seminar following their student teaching experience are paired with students just starting their teaching experience. The senior students observed their student teacher six times during the semester, providing peer support and feedback. Also, the seniors were expected to discuss their tutoring experience, as well as their own student teaching experience, in the seminar. Based on interviews with tutors and tutees, Riley and Huffman concluded that the peer support experience was valuable to both groups. The student teachers revealed that knowing their peer supporter recently had been through the same experience made it easier to discuss problems:

> *Supported by someone in addition to the university supervisor and cooperating teacher encouraged those beginning student teaching to lose their inhibitions. More talk about teaching and students was the result. The fact that a "recent survivor", a person who had been in a similar situation, was working with them was encouraging. Success in this internship experience might be within their reach as well* (Riley and Huffman 1980, p. 11).

In addition, the *peer tutors* reported that, besides sharpening their observation skills and becoming more aware of teaching alternatives, the experience of tutoring was highly motivating:

> *In the typical teaching program, student teachers who interned successfully during the fall semester return to the university in spring saddened. They talk of missing their classrooms, appear to be less involved in their university*

studies, and are anxious to obtain a position. The opportunity to be a peer support person seemed to minimize the commonly experienced separation pains, for as peer support people they were involved directly in classrooms and with students, simply in a different role. The realization that someone depended upon them for assistance was a motivator and increased their confidence in their own skills (Riley and Huffman 1980, pp. 10-11).

The use of *peer tutors* to enrich a practicum also has been used in the field of industrial engineering. At West Virginia University, a teacher (Bailey 1986) organized a program in which entering sophomore students were assigned to work unpaid one day a week for nine months in a West Virginia corporation as industrial engineers. Each student was assigned to a senior student who had survived the rigors of the curriculum to provide personal and academic advice. By having someone more experienced to talk with, the new students could discuss and debrief their workplace experience. In turn, the older students gained the experience of being mentors and motivators.

Clearly, it seems appropriate for students learning a new skill, for example, teaching, to be tutored by students who recently learned this skill. This concept has been applied to nursing skills by Cason, Cason, and Bartnick (1977), who arranged for new students learning patient care skills to begin by observing a more advanced student. Then the advanced student observed the beginner try the same skill, providing feedback and guidance. When both the tutor and the tutee feel ready, they ask a faculty member to test the student in front of the peer teacher. After demonstration of basic mastery of the skill by the learner, the *peer teacher* instructs finer points of the task.

The benefit to the *peer teacher* when a skill is to be taught is expressed in the dictum, *"See one, do one, teach one"* (Schwenk and Whitman 1987, p. 136). In a discussion of teaching clinical skills to medical students and residents, Schwenk and Whitman also addressed the benefit to the learner being taught by a more advanced peer: Peers can be aware of the level of sophistication at which the learner is functioning and can match their teaching at that level. Sometimes, faculty teach at a level of understanding that is higher, or lower, than the student's, which can be unproductive and/or frustrating. However, peer teachers who recently have learned a skill themselves teach at the right level.

At the University of Nebraska at Omaha, upper division students who had mastered basic Spanish language skills conducted three or four supplemental sessions for students in the beginning level course. In the pilot program, 20 of 97 students voluntarily attended these tutorials. Although the staff reported that benefits far outweighed problems, student tutors were prone to time conflicts as the demands of midterms, finals, and term papers interfered with the tutors' ability to meet time commitments (Harrington and Moore 1986).

In contrast to the aforementioned examples of using *peer tutors* who share a similar interest with their tutees, but differ only in level of accomplishment, the Science Mentor Program at Brown University links students with dissimilar interests. In science courses with enrollments over 100, up to 20 nonscience majors were invited to attend an additional weekly group meeting led by undergraduate science majors as well as the course instructor. The science mentors acted as tutors as well as teaching assistants, serving as peer advisors on a one-to-one basis, monitoring the progress of their students and trying to clarify course content (Heywood 1988).

Peer tutoring can be an effective remedy for students in academic difficulty. For example, in 1978 the University of Texas Medical Branch at Galveston implemented a peer tutoring system to help students with deficient grades (C or below) in basic science courses (Trevino and Eiland 1980). The tutors included doctoral students in the Graduate School of Biomedical Sciences, and junior and senior medical students. At the end of two terms, the grades of tutored students were reviewed. Fifty-five freshmen and sophomore students were tutored, eight in more than one subject. As a group, these students *increased* their mean tests scores from 69 to 76. The minimum passing score was 74. Unfortunately, the investigators did not report how many students removed the deficient grade. Also, while the students being tutored responded in a survey that the tutorial program was worthwhile, the authors did not report whether there were differences in the tutoring by graduate students versus fellow medical students.

The University of Maryland School of Medicine also implemented a *peer tutoring system* to help students having difficulty with basic science courses (Walker-Bartnick, Berger, and Kappelman 1984). In their program, sophomores, juniors, and seniors who had done well in these courses tutored freshmen and sophomores. In its first year (1981–82), 25 tutors helped 38 students, and in the second year (1982–83), 33 tutors helped 46 students. For both academic years, 10 students being tutored failed one course, and two students failed two courses. Three students were dismissed academically. Unfortunately, the authors did not provide data for previous academic years to measure the impact of the tutoring system on course failures and academic dismissals; however, they reported that the overall impact on students with academic difficulty was positive. In addition, they reported benefits to the tutors, including the opportunity to review material for standardized examinations required for medical licensing.

Counselors

Peer counselors are similar to *peer tutors*. Both are *near-peers*, working with students on a one-to-one basis. However, while the objective of a tutor is to help improve a student's performance in a specific course, the focus of a *counselor* is more general. Although some counseling programs use the term "tutor" for their peer teachers, this higher education report will consider them *"counselors"* if their focus is general. Another way this difference can be seen is in the peer teacher's affiliation. Tutors work with a course director and help students enrolled in that course. *Counselors* work in a counseling center and work with students regardless of course enrollment. The variety of ways in which students counsel fellow students was discussed in a comprehensive review. Presenting case studies in peer counseling at Florida State University, the review described a wide variety of services, including telephone crisis intervention, curriculum and career information programs, and academic counseling (Austin 1982).

This higher education report reviews peer counseling programs aimed at helping students improve academic performance. For example, at Stanford University, a Learning Assistance Center helps students having trouble with study skills, irrespective of the content of any particular course. Students seeking help are encouraged to try to get assistance for specific problems from their instructors and department consulting centers. But, when the problems seem too large, or too general, to be dealt with effectively at the department level, the center assigns the student a *student counselor*. These counselors are all Stanford students, generally upperclassmen who have completed the introductory courses. Roughly half of the students who would like to be tutors are selected, and they take a training course which is offered for one credit hour. This course addresses counseling skills, common learning blocks, and effective study skills. In a typical year, a class of 25 to 30 counselors will help 350 students (Walker, Von Bargen, and Wessner 1980).

At Middlesex County College in Edison, New Jersey, the Career-Oriented Peer Tutoring System (COPS) was developed to reach potentially unsuccessful entering freshmen students, offering scholastic remedial work and vocational information. This program was initiated by a report by the Student Retention Committee that, typically, 60 percent of new students were leaving Middlesex by the end of the third semester. However, only 12 percent of those leaving left due to academic dismissal. Most left for personal and other reasons, including their feeling that they did not fit in. To reduce attrition, the college staff hoped that peer counselors could make a difference: "Feelings of alienation, poor communication skills, lack of direction, and a sense of being a number rather than an individual were areas of stress that positive contacts with peers could alleviate" (Thomas 1982, p. 8).

Using advertising, faculty referrals, and honor society rosters, approximately 30 counselors were hired, trained, and actively functioning during the 1981–82 school year. Training included workshops on the goals and objectives of the project, role playing of typical student problems, and orientation to campus resources. In the first year, 220 students received help in 72 courses. Math–related subjects exceeded all others in numbers of students assisted, resulting in an increased hiring of tutors in the math and business division. Counseling seemed to have a positive impact on pass-fail rates; in every course but Business Math and Developmental Math I, the percent of tutored students passing the course *exceeded* the passing rate of the total enrollment. Most faculty reported that they thought students benefited; and subjective interpretation by the project staff, based on anecdotal information, was that both peer teachers and learners benefited. Specifically, *peer teachers* reported that they liked the chance to review course content and enjoyed helping others, and the *learners* expressed a strong wish to interact and learn from successful students. Unfortunately, long-term attrition rates were not reported in the published report (Thomas 1982).

The two-year Ongentz Campus of Pennsylvania State University developed another program to address the problems of academically underprepared students. Its Writing Center, staffed by paid *peer tutors*, helps students in any courses. Recruitment of *peer tutors* for the coming academic year begins in the previous spring term when faculty in the English department recommend students who have successfully completed two composition courses. Usually, 15 to 20 names are submitted to the director of the Writing Center, who discusses the strengths and weaknesses of each student with the recommending teacher in order to rank the prospective counselors. Then the director interviews each candidate, reviewing three or four papers from the previous composition courses. The objectives of the interview are to determine if the student has the necessary attributes to be a *peer tutor*, and to familiarize candidates with the peer tutoring program. The main attributes of an effective counselor in this program include the ability to communicate well with peers and to be sensitive to students' problems. Based on these considerations, students, who themselves were counseled in the Writing Center, may be selected as *peer tutors*, as well as superior students who had no such need (Rizzolo 1982).

Typically, four to eight students are chosen at Ongentz, and they participate in a three–week, four hours a week, internship during which a *senior tutor* is assigned to each *new tutor* to orient the newcomers to the Writing Center and the tutor's responsibility. Thus, peer teaching is used to train the peer teachers. In the internship, center staff and experienced peer teachers emphasize that the role of the *peer tutor* is to facilitate, not to proofread. Nevertheless, the director reports that new tutors tend to want to do all the work for the students they are supposed to be helping, and "almost instinctively fall into the familiar pattern of the active teacher-passive student, a pattern rooted in the 'sponge' method of learning: Listen and soak up" (Rizzolo 1982, p. 118).

By the end of the fall term, however, *counselors* in the Writing Center become more comfortable with engaging students in analyzing their own work, asking questions such as:

- What was your specific assignment?
- How did you go about doing it?
- What is your main idea (thesis statement)?
- Can you underline it in the paper?
- What ideas did you use to develop your main idea?
- Can you bracket them?

- Can you point out important details? (Rizzolo 1982, p. 118).

Using informal evaluation, the director meets individually with tutors on a weekly basis, providing positive feedback and reinforcing effective practices. Based on feedback from students who are helped and from their faculty, Rizzolo concluded that *peer teachers*, while not providing the complete answer to assisting underprepared students, can be an effective method to cultivate a genuine concern for sound writing in all courses among a sizeable portion of the student body.

The Ongentz writing center is one of many *peer counseling programs* aimed at improving writing skills through student collaboration. A *pioneer* in the student collaboration movement is Kenneth Bruffee, a founder in the early 1970s of the Brooklyn College Writing Center, which is a model used by other institutions. In short, the "Brooklyn Plan" makes expository writing the focus of peer influence. When the project began, Brooklyn College had a Writing Center staffed by professionally trained counselors. However, few students used it and it was not very helpful to those who did. After training students to become *counselors*, the Writing Center began to average 1,000 tutoring encounters per term (Bruffee 1978).

An unexpected result was the effect on *peer teachers*:

There (was) nothing in the literature on peer teaching which would lead us to expect that average and somewhat above average undergraduates acting as tutors could develop so rapidly through a process of peer influence a capacity so essential to mature thought (Bruffee 1978, p. 451).

A benefit of peer-mediated writing programs is that faculty in any discipline may be encouraged to make writing assignments without having to become writing teachers themselves. For example, the Writing Fellows Program at Brown University helps support a writing-across-the curriculum effort. Undergraduate *counselors* serve over 3,000 students a year (Romer 1985).

Our understanding of how *student counselors* can help improve writing skills has been deepened by the requirement at the University of California, Berkeley Student Learning Center, that they keep journals to describe their efforts. The *peer teachers* are juniors and seniors who get academic credit in the

Peer Teachers, while not providing the complete answer to assisting underprepared students, can be an effective method to cultivate a genuine concern for sound writing in all courses.

School of Education for helping freshmen and sophomores coming to the center for help on papers they are writing for courses. In reviewing the journals, Hawkins found that *student counselors* provide a link between the writer and the audience which is often missing when students feel they are writing only for teachers. His interpretation of the peer journals was that the personal contact between the *peer teacher* and *learner* accounted for the success of the program.

> *A peer, unlike a teacher, is still living in the undergraduate experience. Thus, tutor and tutee are more likely to see each other as equals and to create an open, communicative atmosphere, even though the peer tutor is a more advanced student (Hawkins 1980, p. 66).*

Partnerships
Teaching assistants, tutors, and *counselors* are categorized as *"near-peers"* because, although the peer teachers are more advanced than the learners, they are close to their level of education. The fourth and fifth types of peer teachers, *partnerships* and *work groups,* are categorized as *"co-peers"* because the students are at the same level and the roles of teacher and learner are interchangeable. The students teach each other. *Partnerships* refer to one-to-one relationships in which two students interact as teacher and learner.

Marcel Goldschmid is an innovator in the use of student partnerships to teach each other. He developed *"learning cells"* at McGill University. The learning cell is a "dyadic" unit in which partners mutually teach and learn from each other. In this cooperative form of learning in pairs, students alternate asking and answering questions on commonly read materials (Goldschmid 1971). In this arrangement, students read assigned materials and write their own questions in advance of class. At the beginning of class, they are assigned randomly to pairs and take turns asking and answering questions. During this time, the teacher may go from pair to pair, giving feedback and assisting, if necessary. As an alternative, Goldschmid has suggested that students read different materials, teaching what was read to a partner before asking questions. Goldschmid (1970) evaluated the effectiveness of *learning cells* in a large psychology class in which four methods were compared: seminar, discussion, independent study, and learning cell. Students in the learning cells performed significantly better on an unannounced examination and on the final comprehensive examination. In experimental conditions, researchers tested the *learning cell* arrangement and found it effective:

> *What are the attributes of peer-assisted learning that might account for the results observed in these studies? One obvious factor is that studying together in a learning cell provides active practice of the subject matter and immediate feedback for self-evaluation. A second factor is that students studying in learning cells are highly motivated. Students enjoy studying together, and their study behavior is reinforced by increased perceived learning and higher grades. A third factor is that the learning cell participants develop responsibility, not only for their own learning but for the achievement of a valued partner. Lastly, the learning cell seems to provide an effective environment for learning how to learn* (Alexander et al 1974, p. 185).

"Co-peer" partnerships also are used frequently to improve writing skills. The theoretical underpinnings for students helping each other with writing were expressed by Moffett (1968), who stated that, ideally, students should write because they are intent on saying something to an audience. A fellow student provides such an audience. Moreover, another student can provide helpful feedback: *"A student responds and comments to a peer more in his own terms, whereas the teacher is more likely to focus too soon on technique"* (Moffett 1968, p. 193). While students might discount the comments of a teacher ("English teachers are nit-pickers, anyway"), they may feel more obligated to accommodate feedback from a fellow student. Finally, the benefit of giving, as well as getting, feedback is acknowledged. "By habitually responding and coaching, students get insights about their own writing" (Moffett 1968, p. 193).

It is worth noting here that collaborative writing can be conducted in groups as well as in pairs. Students working in groups can discuss and choose promising topics, generate details about each potential topic, and clarify the focus of these topics: *"Five sets of eyes and five brains can locate more patterns, sub-points, potential theses, and interesting editorial slants than can any one writer"* (Gebhardt 1980, p. 73). In addition to the cognitive benefits of collaborative writing, student partners or groups can provide emotional support:

"It is not hard to imagine how crippling the mixture of frustration, loneliness, lack of confidence, and fear of failing can be for students—especially those with limited experience with printed words, those who have had few opportunities to write, those who have received plenty of humiliation at the hand of English teachers" (Gebhardt 1980, p. 71).

Student partnerships are used in a two-semester course in critical thinking at Westfield State College (Massachusetts), where freshmen students are required to edit each other's writing assignments. The *"peer editor"* must make comments on a fellow student's draft and OK each section. This peer editing gives additional feedback to students on the quality of their work before they turn it in for a grade and fosters cooperation between students (Rasool and Tatum 1988).

The peer editing process acts as a means of having the students share the reality of an academic environment. The editors must collude with us in being part of the scholarly community. They must now take a critical look at one of their peer's essays. They must share in the experience of evaluating an essay and in giving that peer some feedback about the essay (Rasool and Tatum 1988, p. 38).

Jacko (in Moffett 1968) extended the concept of dyadic partnerships to triads in which students exchange first drafts of their papers and provide each other with feedback. More recently, Benesch also looked at three-member peer groups, specifically in a freshmen composition course (1985). In order to find out what was discussed during their meetings, she taped their conversations, with student permission. In addition to discussion of their drafts ("text talk"), and social chat ("off-task talk"), students also talked about the assignment and the course-in-general ("metaresponse"). The metaresponse of students, which included an opportunity to vent frustrations about the course, provided a "hidden benefit" of peer writing instruction (Benesch 1985, p. 9).

A researcher taped student response groups to find out whether the benefits of student collaboration could be charted over a semester. By the fourth week of the semester, students began to examine their own drafts for considerations other than surface errors: "Students began to 'resee' their own drafts" (Coleman 1987, p. 8). Students

*had moved farther away from being inexperienced writers
and were doing more of the kinds of things that experienced
writers do—experiencing dissonance, doing more self-moni-
toring, and beginning to write passionately and read criti-
cally* (Coleman 1987, p. 12).

In the words of a student, *"The paper was talking back"* (p. 12).

While much research on the effectiveness of peer-mediation
in the teaching of writing has involved native speakers of English, Hvitfeldt (1986) found in her literature review that research on *peer teaching* with writers of English as a second
language (ESL) was inconclusive. Moreover, her attempts with
peer teaching with ESL have met with varying degrees of success. However, if students are given very specific guidelines to
follow, peer ESL teachers can be helpful. At a branch campus
of Indiana University in Malaysia, student partnerships were
used in an English course for students who had finished two
years of college training conducted in the national language,
Bahasa Malaysia (Hvitfeldt 1986). The purpose of the ESL
course is to prepare students to finish the last two years of a
bachelor's degree at Indiana University. In the course, the first
draft of each student's essay is distributed randomly to another
student and is critiqued at the next class session. The *peer re-
viewers* are asked to read their classmate's essay carefully and
to answer questions on a peer critique form. Rewriting is conducted at the next class, where the writer may ask questions of
both the peer teacher and the course teacher. Hvitfeldt's personal impression is that the real value of these student partnerships *"appears to be in the doing rather than the receiving"*
(1986, p. 5). In other words, often it is the *peer teacher* who
learns the most from peer teaching:

> *Responding to their classmates' essays forces the students to
> interact through writing and emphasizes the importance of
> writing for an audience. Yes, peer critique is time consum-
> ing. Yes, student feedback is sometimes vague, incomplete,
> or even mistaken. Yet peer critique offers the students an op-
> portunity to develop their own critical reading skills with
> material that is at their own language level. It also functions
> as the first step in learning to look at their own writing more
> critically at the rewriting stage* (Hvitfeldt 1986, p. 5)

In addition to *"co-peer"* partnerships in the teaching of Eng-

lish as a second language, "co-peer" work groups also have been used in ESL courses. The fifth type of peer teaching in higher education, work groups, will begin with a description of peer work groups used in a Swedish undergraduate course in English as a second language.

Work Groups

Student work groups were used in a Swedish undergraduate course in the English department of Linkoping University. During the prewriting stage, students working in groups brainstormed topic ideas and helped each other develop outlines. After a first draft, students critiqued each other's work, responding to the ideas, presentation, and language used in their essays. According to the course developers, the main advantages of students working in groups included:

1. Saving teachers' time from editing tasks, thus freeing them to spend more time for more helpful guidance and instruction
2. Providing feedback from fellow students, which might be perceived as more helpful than from teachers
3. Using multiple readers which may give students a sense of a wider audience
4. Enhancing student attitudes towards writing as a result of socially supportive peers
5. Learning more about writing by having to read and edit each others' written work (Davies and Omberg 1986).

Based on student responses to surveys, researchers concluded that student work groups were perceived by students as an important complement to the curriculum. Students did not propose that peer groups replace the instructors, but did suggest additional uses of peer support, including discussion of assigned books. Overall, students reported that work groups provided welcomed social contact and a sense of security:

Apart from the respect which group work inspires for the process of writing and the undoubted consequent improvement in the final product, it encourages the stimulation of ideas, and the build up of confidence. It fosters intellectual exchange, a critical sense and the ability to give and take criticism, also to play the teacher role to some extent. The experience of mutual help and inspiration has an important

*social value, especially for students who have not known
each other for long* (Davies and Omberg 1986, p. 15).

Social goals also were the aim of a peer group effort at Im-
perial College in London, England. Here, an attempt was made
to tackle the problem with the engineering curriculum where
students felt isolated during the first year when there is a heavy
emphasis on learning basic information through large lectures.
Textbooks and supplementary notes replaced lectures. Students
were placed in groups of six to eight who were instructed in an
experimental procedure by a video tape. Each group of students
carried out the experiment, and groups met afterwards to compare and discuss results. Two teachers circulated among
groups, offering guidance where necessary. But, the idea was
for students to help each other (Jacques 1984).

Do instructional objectives suffer when student work groups
are formed to meet social objectives? Studies comparing students in self-directed small groups to students in large lectures
demonstrate little difference in objective test results (Beach
1974). In some studies, the self-directed small group students
actually test better, but not at a statistically significant level.
The demonstrated social benefits include increased communica-
tive and interpersonal skills, as well as greater enthusiasm for
learning.

Another question raised by student work groups is whether
students should be assigned randomly or matched. To supplement a large lecture course in an upper division Abnormal Psychology course at the University of Hawaii, Diamond (1972)
matched 104 students into 20 heterogeneous groups of five to
six students each. Students were matched based on student survey data: each group was composed of an advanced, and successful, volunteer leader plus a mix of students who differed in
psychology background and orientation. Students were instructed to meet weekly on their own, and to arrange their own
meeting time and place. The structure of each group was left to
the group's discretion, and the course instructor and graduate
teaching assistants were available for guest consultations. Each
group was required to submit four discussion essays and take
an essay final examination. Over 90 percent of the students
perceived the group meeting and requirements favorably. In
comparison to end of the semester evaluations completed by
students in the rest of the university, students in this course reported a statistically significant greater level of participation,

greater social and personal development, and more student interaction. In addition, enhanced thinking was significant statistically. While data indicates that small, heterogeneous student-led discussion groups are perceived by students as an asset to a large undergraduate lecture course, generalizations concerning the groups' facilitation of learning can not be made on the basis of this study. Assignment of students to student-led, homogeneous groups and to teacher-led groups would make the results more generalizable.

A comparison of an experimental with a control group was provided by researchers who organized students in two introductory classes into two groups (Slotnick, Jeger, and Schure 1981). *Students in the experimental group* (N—50) were divided into networks of four persons. They met once a week in lieu of the regular lecture, and working together, studied course material and prepared for examinations. The professor and teaching assistant circulated among the networks to facilitate cooperative work and help maintain the group's task orientation. *Students in the control group* (N—29) attended the regular lecture. The two groups were comparable on variables such as age, sex, academic ability, and major distribution, as well as on performance on the first quiz administered prior to selecting the experimental class.

By three academic measures (six biweekly quizzes, a midterm exam, and a final exam), the students in the experimental group performed better at a statistically significant level. Not surprisingly, they also performed better on a networking and a social climate assessment. The networking was measured by the ability of students to know other students in the course by name, and the social climate was measured by the Classroom Environment Scale developed by Moos and Trickett (Slotnick, Jeger, and Schure 1981). Despite these positive results, the authors acknowledged some *negative* features associated with the program. Some students assigned to the experimental group felt anxious about participating in self-directed sessions in lieu of the lectures, and viewed the networks as a shirking of teacher responsibility, *"espousing the belief that only the legitimate professional authority can deliver 'officially authentic' education"* (Slotnick, Jeger, and Schure 1981, p. 7). Of course, these complaints could have been avoided if the students had self-selected into the experimental or control groups. But then the investigators would have introduced a bias into the study.

Several successful efforts to use student work groups have

been reported in medical schools. Researchers described the use of *student teams* in a sophomore patient-interviewing and clinical problem-solving course at Northeastern Ohio University (Pepe, Hodel, and Bosshart 1980). The medical students are video taped interviewing simulated patients, and fellow students provide critique. A *cooperative learning group approach* for freshmen medical students in the biochemistry laboratory course at the University of Minnesota was implemented, in which the grade for each student was dependent upon the single grade given to the total small group's work (Roon et al 1983). *Reciprocal Peer Teaching* was used in a gross anatomy laboratory course at the University of Ottawa in which students in small groups took turns taking responsibility for teaching topics (Hendelman and Boss, 1986). In all these uses of work groups in medical schools, the students reported liking the opportunity to develop teaching skills that could be applied to communicating with patients.

One of the best known medical student programs that incorporates *peer teaching* is McMaster University. Here, there is a stated objective for each student *"to become a self-directed learner, recognizing personal educational needs, selecting appropriate learning resources, and evaluating progress"* (Ferrier, Marrin, and Seigman 1988). At McMaster University, the medical education program is based on a problem-based method where students work in a sequence of small groups. The students are responsible for facilitating the learning and evaluating of their peers, and they are expected to be challenging and critical of each other, as well as supportive. A similar model of teaching was initiated in 1986 at Harvard Medical School in a program known as the "New Pathway," in which student groups discuss simulated patient problems. Students are expected to seek relevant information independently and to share what they have discovered.

Summary
Five types of peer teaching are used in higher education.

- *Near-peer* teaching includes teachers who are more advanced than their learners, but still are peers: undergraduate teaching assistants, tutors, and counselors.
- *Co-peer* teaching includes teachers who are at the same level as their learners: partnerships and work groups.

The purpose of all five types of *peer teaching* is to satisfy needs that much traditional schooling leaves unfulfilled, rather than promote the agenda of traditional schooling. *Peer teaching* assumes that what students should learn includes *effective inter-dependence* and *social maturity*, and it postulates that *social maturity* and *intellectual maturity* are inseparable.

An excellent description, analysis, and theoretical discussion of the various types of peer teaching in higher education noted that, to some teachers, the idea of students taking on a teaching function may conflict with their assumption that teaching is, by definition, the prerogative of the teacher (Cornwall 1979). So, when considering the implementation of *peer teaching programs*, academic planners should anticipate whether there will be resistance to change. An associate dean has found much skepticism about using undergraduate teaching assistants among faculty who have never used them. However, she has not encountered faculty who have worked with undergraduate teaching assistants no longer using them because they were ineffective. At Brown University, a researcher thought that a source of skepticism may be that faculty who have never worked with undergraduate teaching assistants may assume that they are doing exactly what graduate assistants would do. Thus, using undergraduate teaching assistants would mean not only taking a job away from graduate students, but also replacing them with less knowledgeable persons (Romer 1988).

The need to define clearly the role of peer teachers also has been identified. . .as a key to winning support and to ensuring program success.

The concern that peer teachers may be replacing *"real"* teachers was encountered at Athabasca University in Edmonton, Alberta, Canada, where program planners were surprised by the resistance of faculty. Athabasca University operates a "distance education" program for off-campus students. Based on a literature review, administrators believed that *peer teaching* would be ideal in this setting because *peer tutors* who already had completed a course would be in a good position to understand what it takes to be a successful distance learner. In addition, peer teachers would not have to spend large amounts of time studying the course to know it in detail, and using course credit or stipends would save money (Coldeway 1980). Although the pilot program included a tutor for an English course and a social science course, objections raised in the social science department caused the *peer tutor* to withdraw before the experiment began. Although peer teaching appeared to be warranted by the program planners, the negative reaction of the staff came as a surprise:

> At the heart of the staff resistance to peer tutoring are concerns for the preservation of "regular, part-time tutors," and their perceived need for "professional" tutors who have corresponding degree credentials. Even though the stated goal of the proposed peer tutoring research program clearly

indicated that an objective examination to determine if and how peer tutors functioned and performed would occur, a large number of staff indicated that they were not in favor of even experimenting with peer tutoring and had little interest in the results. They also expressed concern that if and when peer tutoring was found to be more and/or equally effective as regular tutoring, the regular tutoring system would be eliminated by university administration in an effort to reduce costs. The replacement peer tutoring system, even though potentially as effective, would be viewed by students and others as nonprofessional and therefore discredit the university (Coldeway 1980, pp. 10–11).

In his analysis of the resistance to change, Coldeway said that the regular tutoring system had not been evaluated carefully before experimenting with peer tutoring, and that the role of professional versus student tutors had not been well-defined. The need to define clearly the role of peer teachers also has been identified by other program planners as a key to winning support and to ensuring program success. For example, for peer teaching to work in writing centers, it is essential that student tutors not become teachers writ small (Bruffee 1978). The peer teachers, themselves, may have difficulty understanding that they are not replacing regular teachers:

Because they have long been trained in the passive "reception of information" and in "success through competition" students may need to be inducted to the academic and social skills necessary for peer tutoring (Jacques 1984, p. 108).

If the nature of peer teaching is not clear to faculty and students, and if they interpret the meaning of peer teaching differently, then academic planners could expect resistance to change. The key to overcoming resistance is to deal with the causes, not its symptoms. Thus, peer teaching advocates should consider establishing two-way communication, allowing others an opportunity to air their feelings, involving them in data collection, and providing opportunities to participate in the implementation (Zander 1962). Questions which administrators should be prepared to answer include:

- *What will it cost in time and money?*
- *What are the potential risks as well as benefits?*

- *How does this program relate to our institution's goals and objectives?*
- *Where did this idea come from?*
- *Can it be tried out first on a small scale?* (Craig 1978)

Key issues to be considered in advance of implementation include public relations, the recruitment and selection of peer teachers, and development of a training program for peer teachers. The experiences of staff who already have implemented peer teaching programs can be helpful to staff who are planning new peer teaching efforts.

Public Relations

The importance of presenting a good image to students, faculty, and administration was noted by the peer teaching program director at the Community College of the Finger Lakes, Canandaigua, New York, who recommends an advertising campaign to recruit tutors and clients. Posters, flyers, newspaper blurbs, and presentations to student clubs can be used to recruit tutors, using the help of students from marketing class if college facilities are lacking. To prevent faculty resistance, garner their support at department meetings and through personal, informal conversations with faculty leaders (Starks 1984). In order to present a positive image to the college administration, it may be helpful to compile reports from the evaluation process. For example, at Finger Lakes, the peer tutoring program coordinator files a report with the college administration about the number of students served, hours tutored, budget, and a comparison of grades received in tutored courses. This information has been helpful in getting college-wide support both from faculty and administration (Starks 1984).

Other caveats learned in operating the peer tutoring program at Finger Lakes include the importance of (a) putting rules and policies in writing so that goals and objectives of the program are not misunderstood, and (b) orienting and training tutors so that their role is understood (Starks 1984). Public relations also was emphasized as a key ingredient in the success of the Career Oriented Peer Tutoring System at Middlesex County College. To win faculty cooperation and college-wide understanding, the project coordinator met with academic deans, department chairpersons, and individual faculty members. In these meetings, the project coordinator explained the program's objectives and emphasized the need for strong working relationships between faculty, tutors, and tutees. Publicity included posters on campus, an article and advertisement in the student newspaper, and promotional spots on the college radio station (Thomas 1982). Of course, the best public relations is the good news spread by a successful program. The final report of the tutoring system at Middlesex County College (1982) concluded:

> *The stimulus to the college community due to the program is an area that needs further study. Increased curiosity and interest by the faculty developed throughout the year. Publicity and word of mouth information brought an awareness of what was being attempted. Faculty members referred students for both tutoring and to be tutors. Any increased involvement by the college faculty would add to the students' chances to feel at home and to succeed in the school environment* (Thomas 1982, p. 80).

Recruitment and Selection

In addition to alerting the academic community-at-large, a specific purpose of a public relations campaign may be to recruit potential peer teachers. To create a successful tutoring and advising program, staff at Middlesex County College needed to hire a broad representation of the school population. To recruit sophomores from across the curriculum, staff used advertisements, faculty referrals, and honor society rosters to produce a file of potential tutors and advisors. Prospects were invited to apply, and their academic records and references were checked prior to a personal interview (Thomas 1982).

By and large, faculty referrals are the most common means of recruitment. In the emulated "Brooklyn Plan," prospective peer tutors are recommended by the English department (Deming 1986). At the Learning Assistance Center at Stanford University, residence hall staff as well as faculty are asked to recommend counselors. Students who are nominated, or who nominate themselves, are asked to complete an application form and to describe why they think they are qualified. All candidates are interviewed by both the program and assistant program director. Generally, there are twice as many applicants as the program needs and selection is made on the basis of demand in certain subject areas, the students' academic record, references, and the personal interviews (Walker, Von Bargen, and Wessner 1980).

Program planners should consider a written job description to guide the recruitment and selection process. The following job description is used in the Special Services Program at Wichita State University aimed to provide tutorial assistance to disadvantaged students. Being specific can help interested students decide whether they really want to be peer teachers and can help staff select suitable students.

The tutor-advisor is responsible for the delivery of tutorial services to project students on a one-to-one basis. Tutor-advisors are students currently attending WSU and are required to have a minimum cumulative GPA of 3.0 or 3.0 in specific subjects tutored. Tutor-advisors are selected for competency in specific subject areas, interest and awareness of problems facing the economically disadvantaged student and willingness to serve as a role model for academic success. They must be sensitive to the students' needs and be able to communicate well and relate meaningfully to fellow students. Tutor-advisors are responsible for reporting to the program counselors. Daily attendance sign-in and attendance at the weekly meeting with the program counselors are required. Contact slips of tutoring sessions are required for each student that the tutor-advisor meets with during each week (deSilva and Freund 1985, p. 17).

In recruiting and selecting students for ''co-peer'' programs in which students teach each other, faculty may need to emphasize the need for students to become cooperative, rather than competitive. Faculty should convey to student participants that their goal is to become responsible for the learning of classmates, rather than to beat them in grades (Goldschmid 1976). On the other hand, in ''near-peer'' programs, the peer teachers are expected to be more advanced than the students they teach. Therefore, grades in the particular subject to be taught, or the overall academic achievement of the peer teacher, are important. However, academic achievement alone does not predict success in peer teaching. For example, at Malcolm X College in Chicago tutors are expected to be people-oriented as well as knowledgeable. Thus, in addition to having earned an A or B in the course they plan to tutor, students are chosen on the basis of their ability to get along cooperatively with classmates. In selecting peer teachers at Malcolm X College, Williams looks for students whom other students question in the classroom (1981).

The key to effective recruitment and selection of peer teachers lies in faculty looking out for *potential* peer teachers in their classrooms. Which students seek to understand the material presented in the course rather than memorize it? Which students respect and listen to the views of fellow students? Which students seek collaboration and see learning as a social process? Recruitment of peer teachers can begin with faculty feedback to students that they should consider participating in the institution's peer teaching efforts. The possibility of becoming a peer teacher may foster increased learning by providing a new, not before considered, focus for a student.

Training

Peer teaching administrators universally emphasize the need for orientation and training. Basically, there are two types of training programs described in the literature: those in which peer teachers are trained in a college course, and those in which they are trained outside a formal class session. In the peer writing program at Brooklyn College, peer tutors are enrolled in an intermediate composition course before tutoring in the beginning course. The major emphasis of the intermediate course is to teach students how to improve their own writing, as well as how to give criticism to fellow students. As an example of a less formal approach, the University of Cincinnati provides role playing sessions for tutors in which they take turns assuming the roles of client, critic, and observer. Informal role playing also is used to train tutors at New York University where the focus of training is on interpersonal communication skills. A combination of formal and informal methods are used at Berkeley where, through a course sponsored by the School of Education, tutors are trained through seminars and video taped sessions (Deming 1986).

At Stanford University, the Learning Assistance Center offers its own course, "Peer Teaching Techniques," in which students meet one hour a week in a seminar format to discuss reading material. Topics include tutoring theory, common problem-solving blocks, and effective learning and studying skills. Video tapes of tutoring sessions are shown and critiqued, and most tutors describe this training as indispensable (Walker, Von Bargen, and Wessner 1980).

As part of its peer training program, the Writing/Reading

Center at Southeastern Massachusetts University conducts a video tape production workshop following a series of seminars on teaching methods, how to help students with writing and reading skills, and how to use the library as a resource. In the video tape workshop, experienced tutors plan, write, and act in a video production to show new tutors situations that may occur in peer teaching. Short skits are used to illustrate approaches to tutoring and overplayed wrong ways are acted out to provide humor (Glassman 1984). Peer teachers learn about teaching when they teach new peer teachers how to teach:

> *Tutors who work on the project become better tutors, are given new responsibility and recognition, are given the opportunity to achieve and grow, and feel better about tutoring. As they work on these tapes, the tutors become more aware of how they tutor and how they come across to their students, decide what are the most important ingredients of being a good tutor, define a tutor's role, clarify what they know, and find ways of sharing this knowledge with other students (Glassman 1984, pp. 10–11).*

In contrast to the Southeastern Massachusetts University video taping, which is intended to be an amateur production, a professional approach to video taped training has been used in Merrimack College (Massachusetts) in which the viewer is introduced to the English department's Peer Tutoring Program. Following a program description, several scenarios are portrayed, and four major teaching points are made:

1. *Be attentive. Since the writing center exists to provide assistance on a drop-in or referral basis to any writer who asks for it, you must always be ready to engage the student in a conversation about her writing. The initial meeting therefore is crucial, for if you show indifference, or, worse yet, a lack of interest in the student, she is not likely to come back and make use of the center's services.*
2. *You're a tutor, not a preacher. The tutor's role is a difficult one, but it does not entail preaching. It does involve being aware of the student's needs at all times. You can only help a student writer if you are not oblivious to what he wants to do, and how your skills can accommodate him. It is important, therefore, that you set up an agenda*

with the writer to help him discover a way for achieving his aim and reaching his audience.

3. ***Don't judge or grade.*** *The tutor is an adjunct to the professor, true. But the tutor works on a one-on-one basis with another student about her writing. Since tutors share equal status with student writers, because of their being students, they can help the students see things in a way most instructors cannot.*

4. ***Avoid discussing the grade and never criticize the professor.*** *The tutor is often seen as the student's ally against the professor. Avoid compromising yourself in this manner, for it will only make the student's improvement less steady* (DeCiccio 1986, pp. 4, 7, 13).

Peer teaching training, from the peer teacher's perspective, was described by a student at Colorado State University, a teaching assistant in the psychology department. To become a teaching assistant, students had to have taken the course and also are expected to attend a weekly teaching seminar. Faculty conducted the seminars, and guests invited to share their teaching experiences included the academic vice-president, the dean, and the department head. Key issues addressed in the seminars included how to be a friend and teacher at the same time, and how to deal with the fear that fellow students may not accept the teaching efforts of peers. The peer teacher trainee found the open discussion helpful (Vattano et al. 1973).

Peer Teacher Manuals

As an adjunct to formal and informal training approaches, peer teacher programs often provide manuals to guide their peer teachers. For example, the major purpose of a handbook developed at Wichita State University is to be a simple aid to college students who are tutors to academically disadvantaged students in a Special Services Program. While it is not possible for a single manual to cover all the issues a tutor has to encounter, this tutor handbook includes the most essential resources available to tutors with checklists, follow-up activities, tutoring tips, and steps to plan and structure the tutorial process. Specific topics addressed include stress and time management, study skills, and learning theory (deSilva and Freund 1985).

Based on ten years of experience at the Academic Improvement Center at Metropolitan State College in Denver, Moore and Poppino warn that peer teaching program staff have to emphasize to peer teachers that tutoring is not the same as classroom teaching. To help train tutors, they wrote a handbook, *Successful Tutoring: A Practical Guide to Adult Learning Processes* (1983) that includes exercises which ask readers to think about what they already know about teaching and learning. The handbook's theme is that the role of the tutor is help students learn to learn. To help program planners design and implement peer teaching programs at their institutions, Williams (1981) has written a handbook for administrators, as well as a manual for students. Both documents include a pre- and posttest. The manual for administrators provides an implementation plan, and the manual for students describes learning activities aimed at developing peer teaching skills. For example, the student is asked to read two articles, "The Role of a Community College," and "The Community College Student," and to recall orally on a tape recorder, or write out on paper, the major points of both articles. Then the student is instructed to play the tape or read the paper to a faculty member and discuss it. Although the administrator's and student's manuals were written for the community college setting, educators could modify the materials for other types of institutions.

Systematic Approaches

A self-instructional model developed to help administrators plan and implement a peer teaching program draws upon a review of the literature as well as the educator's own personal experiences. It recommends a five-step process:

1. *"Diagnose and assume the responsibility for correcting the problem."* In other words, is there a need to improve instructional services, and can peer teachers help?
2. *"Define goals and roles."* For example, what is expected of peer teachers, and for what will they be held accountable?
3. *"Eliminate problems and identify additional resources."* Are the peer teachers committed to the program? Will they be paid? What supervision will be provided?
4. *"Determine and select possible solutions."* For instance, how will student clients be identified?
5. *"Implement and evaluate."* Will a formal or informal evaluation be made? Will there be statistical treatment of student outcomes? Will peer teaching sessions be ob-

served? Will peer teachers and students be surveyed? (Williams 1981, pp. 9–13)

Finally, Williams emphasizes that faculty are the key to the successful development and implementation of a peer teaching program. If their involvement is superficial and lacks enthusiasm, the program probably will fail.

Another document aimed at helping administrators also outlined five components essential to a successful peer teaching program at the college level: (1) *organization and funding*, (2) *supervision*, (3) *training*, (4) *program evaluation*, and (5) *public relations* (Starks 1984). Specific suggestions include providing written rules and regulations, tapping funds from a variety of sources (student government, the college foundation, and the regular budget), and involving the faculty in selecting, supervising, and training peer teachers.

Based on their successful peer tutoring program in a medical school, researchers suggested four points to keep in mind when developing a system:

- Screening procedures for tutors are important, including their study habits as well as academic achievement.
- Guidelines for tutors should include a mechanism for regular contact with course directors and written progress reports.
- Collect data on student performance, both tutors and tutees, to evaluate the program.
- Student needs should be assessed and reviewed (Walker-Bartnick, Berger, and Kappelman 1984).

Faculty and administrators interested in planning and developing a peer-supported writing center should consult a book which includes chapters on staffing, program development, and writing a student handbook to supplement training (Olson 1984). In considering the advice of these, and other, program planners, the author wishes to emphasize one recommendation: ***Any plan to reform the university curriculum should include students in the process***. Successful peer teaching requires an assessment by students of their own needs and abilities. Student involvement in the planning process will have long-term, as well as short-term, effects. As pointed out in a primer on reforming educational programs, when university staff collaborate with students in the development of courses and educational policy, more students become interested in academic careers: *"The faculty thus finds itself with a breeding ground for future teaching and research talent and for development of intellectual interests directly related to their own"* (Taylor 1969, p. 325).

Summary

Academic planners considering peer teaching programs should seek to prevent resistance to change and deal with its causes when it occurs. Misunderstanding can be avoided by two-way communication and involvement of the administration, the faculty, and student body. In addition to planning a public relations campaign to present a positive image, staff should consider ahead of time how to recruit, select, and train students to be peer teachers. A systematic approach will increase the likelihood that the program will succeed.

HOW THE CLASSROOM TEACHER CAN IMPLEMENT PEER TEACHING

Aside from campus-wide efforts to plan and conduct peer teaching programs, individual college classroom teachers can use peer teaching to increase student involvement. In this section, faculty efforts to use peer teaching will be described with the aim of providing models for reform-minded teachers. The impetus for reform may be a faculty member's own experience as a college student or teacher. For example, a law professor commented that the stimulus for peer teaching was his own experience of encountering only two courses in college that were real learning experiences. One course was effective because the teacher possessed personal charisma. In the other course, the teacher used a technique referred to as "creative dialogue":

Student-directed discussion groups without adequate structure actually may hinder the learning process.

> *Creative dialogue has at its root the tenet that students are possessed with a great potential to create, that in order for students to create they must also exchange, and that the present lecture system used in most undergraduate courses stifles creativity and exchange* (Tighe 1971, p. 21).

Peer Teaching Experiences

The variation of creative dialogue used by Tighe required that the teacher write questions on the blackboard and instruct students to organize into groups of five or six after the teacher removes himself (or herself) from the classroom. When the teacher leaves, each group selects a spokesperson to record the group's observations and questions and begins discussion. After an hour, the teacher returns and the spokespersons make brief reports. Tighe emphasizes the social process of learning that Bruffee discussed in his essays (1984, 1986).

> *Real learning... is not a solitary task. One person cannot be expected to discover five different interpretations of a piece of literature. But five people can. This is where the real dialogue begins—each student can examine his ideas in relationship to those of his peer group* (Tighe 1971, p. 22).

Another faculty member, a professor of psychology, was motivated to use peer teaching because of his students' reactions to traditional classroom procedures. Grasha, at the University of Cincinnati, interviewed six to 10 students per quarter over a period of two years (1966-68) and found three general responses.

1. The *avoidance* style describes students whose behaviors included cutting classes, noninvolvement in class discussion, and a general lack of interest in taking responsibility for learning.
2. The *competitive* style describes students who enter a course focused on the end product of a good grade rather than on the process of learning, and who view the classroom as grounds for mortal combat.
3. The *dependent* style describes students who seek security by doing what they are told (Grasha 1972).

To overcome these response styles, Grasha implemented a number of reforms in his courses, including giving students responsibility for doing a project of their choice working in small groups of two to five students. Also, they were required to answer study guide questions in small groups, with all the students in a group getting the same grade. In addition, Grasha took responsibility for conducting only 50 to 60 percent of the class sessions, with the remainder run by students. The student *teachers-of-the-day* gave lectures, led discussions, performed demonstrations, or ran experiments. Depending upon the size of the class, students taught alone or in teams.

Based on a quasi-experimental evaluation of the 1970–71 academic year (postcourse surveys of students taking the same courses from Grasha and from a colleague using the traditional lecture and discussion approach), students in the experimental classes judged their behaviors as *less* avoidant, competitive, and dependent. The reforms encouraged students to develop learning skills in addition to acquiring course content (Grasha 1972). The negative responses of students to traditional classes that motivated Grasha to experiment with new classroom procedures also concerned Michaelsen. He observed that in large lecture courses students are forced to be passive, producing apathy, absenteeism, and poor performance. Rather than blaming instructors for poor lecture skills, he tried team learning, in which students are assigned to groups of six or seven members. Looking at team learning in social and physical science courses, Michaelsen found that the process is most effective when groups contain members with a wide variety of viewpoints, and when at least one member has the specific skills necessary for carrying out assigned tasks. For example, in a physical chemistry course, each student group should include both chemistry and engineering majors. Teachers should use questionnaires to identify an appropriate mix of student skills (Michaelsen 1983).

Other peer teaching procedures were developed by Kitchener and Hurst (1972) and evaluated by Arbes and Kitchener (1974). In this case, group leaders were upperclass students who had performed well in the course the previous semester. They were trained to serve as a resource on course content, but not to assume responsibility for directing group discussion. Group discussion participants were instructed to define the key terms and to identify the main theme of a reading assignment. After elaborating on the main theme, students critiqued the author's viewpoint, integrating new information with previously learned material. Finally, students were asked to discuss and evaluate their own group's performance. Student interactions were scored using the Bales' Observation System, and student learning gains were measured on examinations. The results supported the use of student-directed interactions for classroom instruction (Arbes and Kitchener 1974).

The poor performance of a control group that used discussion without an upperclass student resource person, and without a training workshop to orient the student participants to discussion procedures, indicated that student-directed discussion groups without adequate structure actually may hinder the learning process. However, with some structure, teachers can expect students to teach each other, and themselves, in discussion groups without the continued presence of a professor (Arbes and Kitchener 1974). While teachers occasionally may want to attend student-directed sessions and monitor student performance, an issue that emerges for each teacher to address is, *What level of teacher intervention helps or hinders student involvement?*

Whether disgruntled by their own student experience or disappointed by response of students to their courses, faculty who are motivated to experiment with student teams should consult Beach's 1974 review of self-directed student groups and college learning. Factors which she found may interfere with learning include (a) *group members who become overly eager to express themselves and do not listen to each other,* and (b) *no one in the group seems concerned particularly over the group's progress.* Furthermore, factors which may prevent the occurrence of learning include (a) *group members do not read the assigned material,* and (b) *no one reads or studies beyond the reading assignments.*

On the other hand, factors in the group's interaction which may facilitate learning include (a) *group members who link course material to personal examples and life experiences,* and (b) *group members who push beyond the immediate point in the study material and go deeper into the more general and basic issues and questions.* In addition, factors in the group's modus operandi that facilitate learning include: (a) *a student leader who begins by asking other students what notes they took on the reading assignments,* and (b) *group members who discuss ways they could be more effective* (Beach 1974).

Approaches to Peer Teaching
In addition to consulting Beach's review of student discussion groups, faculty should consider the techniques described in *Change* magazine's *Guide to Effective Teaching* (1978). In a section on peer teaching, six approaches are included with specific instructions which can be followed by teachers who wish to incorporate peer teaching in their programs.

• The first approach to peer teaching describes the use by James Maas of *undergraduate teaching assistants* in an introductory psychology course at Cornell University. When Maas started using undergraduate teaching assistants in 1965, enrollment in Psychology 101 was 1,200 and the lectures were held in the university's concert hall. To help personalize the course, Maas recruited upperclassmen to lead one-hour discussion groups once a week. Other faculty were critical, charging that students would complain about the discussion groups because they were *"paying all this money for tuition, and what do they get for a teacher but someone who's only a year or two older, who may or may not be a personal friend"* (Janssen 1978, p. 65). Although his own department was skeptical at first, other faculty in the psychology department began to use undergraduate teaching assistants, as well as faculty in the departments of physics, chemistry, mathematics, and biology.

The key to Maas's success is the selection of teaching assistants (Janssen 1978). Maas, with the help of a graduate assistant, personally selects the teaching assistants. His criteria include that they earned an A− or better in Psychology 101, and hold at least a B+ cumulative average. Applicants must provide faculty recommendations and submit an outline of topics they would like to teach in their sections. If the applicants are not psychology majors, they are expected to have had relevant work experience, in a mental hospital, for example. Maas interviews final candidates: *"I look for the way they speak, to see how nervous they are; an interview is somewhat anxiety-ridden, but then so is teaching. I try to weed out the people who are doing this for ego building"* (Janssen 1978, p. 65).

The job is prestigious and popular; 15 students apply for each opening. Maas invites the new teaching assistants to his house during the summer for an organizing session and meets with them in the fall before classes begin. The teaching assistants are video taped at the beginning, and near the end, of the course. After the first video taping, he meets with teaching assistants individually to give them feedback. They are assigned to two sections in the first year and to three sections, if invited back to teach a second year. In their first year, teaching assistants are given four academic credits, and, in the second year, a waiver of tuition and fees. In the early years, the teaching assistants were expected to review the material covered in the lectures. However, over the years, Maas found better results by allowing teaching assistants the freedom to discuss their own topics. Now the teaching assistants turn in topic lists, and at the first large lecture students choose which discussion group they want to join. The following are examples of topics generated by teaching assistants:

- *Does Familiarity Breed Content or Contempt?* Why do we find some activities more interesting than others? Why do individual preferences differ, or why do they conform? How do our interests differ over time?
- *Psychology and Medicine.* Is there psychosomatic illness? What does the dying patient experience? Does acupuncture work? Should brain surgery be an acceptable practice?
- *Sleep, Dreams, and Sleep-Learning.* Why do some people always seem to sleep well and others poorly? Can sleep-learning be used to break certain habits such as nail-biting?

To judge how the students feel about the undergraduate teaching assistants, Maas administers a questionnaire at the end of each semester. Students tend to report that the teaching assistants seemed knowledgeable, that there was ample opportunity for asking questions, that the discussion sections were interesting, and that they felt that they had learned a lot. In addition, many teaching assistants report that this experience was the highlight of their undergraduate career. Over the years, more than a dozen have gone on to complete doctorate degrees in psychology.

● The second program described in *Change* magazine's peer teaching section is *Bruffee's writing center* at Brooklyn College (Dugger 1978). Dugger's program description is recommended for faculty who wish to train student writing tutors. In selecting trainees to become writing tutors, less emphasis is placed on academic standing compared to teaching assistants. *Being interested in writing is the key criterion*, and some C students as well as B students may make good tutors.

When training tutors, a key issue is the balance between teaching them writing skills versus tutoring skills. At Brooklyn College, the first half of the course for tutors addresses the writing skills of prospective tutors, and the second half focuses on tutoring skills. A stock exercise used at Brooklyn College to teach tutorial skills is evaluation of the "reality paper," a poorly written paper on "God, Reality, and Resignation." Although the students' gut reaction to the paper initially is negative because of its bad grammar, Bruffee tries to help them see through the writing to the author's meaning. After the initial training, writing tutors need additional support. Tutors need to be taught that when they get stuck they should get help. Bruffee comments, "They're taught it's not a humiliation not to know an answer. When they go for help, already they've shown the kid they are working with how to learn" (Dugger 1978, p. 69).

● The third program which may be helpful to teachers is the description of *peer teaching foreign language courses* developed by Howard Lamson at Earlham College in Richmond, Ind. (Sugnet 1978). In Introductory Spanish, French, and German, classes meet for five days a week for three hours a day. In the first hour, students meet in groups of eight to 10 with a student instructor for spontaneous conversation in the foreign language. In the second hour, they meet with the course instructor who introduces new material. In the third hour, students meet in groups of four or five, with a different student instructor than they had for the first hour, to practice in the language laboratory, and to participate in conversation exercises, games, or plays. Peer teachers are students who have successfully completed the introductory course. Although they are paid, the real motivation is their own improvement in foreign language skills and the added contact with college faculty. Student teachers participate in a two-hour workshop before the course begins and in a two-hour seminar once a week during the course. They study theories and methods of language learning and discuss educational issues.

● The fourth approach to peer teaching is a description of Clayton Ladd's program to facilitate *student self-help* groups at Eastern Illinois University (Lincoln 1978). It is recommended for faculty who wish to experiment with student self-help groups. In a course on mental hygiene, Ladd uses students who previously had completed the course to facilitate small group activities. The purpose of the course is to teach self-understanding skills so that students become more aware of their own learning processes and their approaches to coping with everyday life. Although much emphasis is placed on individualized reading and personalized self-help projects, small group sessions, led by students trained to conduct group exercises, are an important element in the course. Student facilitators, in helping their groups carry out the exercises, make additional learning gains themselves.

Since learning gains are made by both learners and teachers in peer teaching programs, it may occur to faculty that peer teaching would be a logical approach for a course on learning. This connection occurred to George Christian Jernstedt at Dartmouth College.

● The fifth approach to peer teaching described by *Change* magazine is based on Jernstedt's Psychology 22: Learning (Egerton 1978). Jernstedt made the teaching of the course an experiment in learning. In fact, a key element of the course is a series of experiments carried out by students designed to illuminate particular principles or concepts. In addition, personal interviews are conducted to allow students to practice what they are learning. Also, students may schedule individual conferences to discuss problems and progress in the course. Finally, students are required to write several one-page briefs. Obviously, it would be difficult, if not impossible, for one instructor to handle these course responsibilities alone.

To assist with course activities, Jernstedt conducts an advanced course for student assistants, Psychology 81: The Teaching-Learning Process in the University. Top students from Psychology 22 are invited to take Psychology 81, and they continue to meet regularly with Jernstedt during Psychology 22. Because up to 200 students at a time take Learning, the course would have to be taught through the traditional method of lectures and examinations if it were not for the student assistants. With the student assistants, it is possible to individualize course activities and to provide a ten to one proctor-student ratio. It would be ironic if a course, whose subject is the learning process, had to violate the principles of learning articulated in it.

• The last program described in *Change* magazine's peer teaching section addresses the *"participatory classroom"* organized by Claire Gaudiani, a French professor at Purdue University (Meeth 1978). To summarize her philosophy of education, she conjugates the verb *apprehendre*, which means both "to teach" and "to learn." The keystone to her course is a personal assessment statement that students complete on the first day of the course, explaining why they have chosen the course, describing their French background, and explaining their strengths and weaknesses.

Students who volunteer that they are timid are offered an arrangement in which Gaudiani promises not to call on them unless they raise their hand; but, they must promise to raise their hands at least once a session. On the other hand, Gaudiani channels the energy of students who like to talk in class. Rather than allowing them to monopolize sessions, she casts them as leaders in preexam review groups and occasionally to team-teach new grammatical concepts. Also, strong and weak students are paired into "study couples."

For faculty who wish to learn more about implementation of peer teaching techniques in the classroom, *Models of Collaboration in Undergraduate Education* (Romer 1985) is recommended because it provides the name, address, and telephone number of a contact person for each program sketched. The programs or projects are categorized according to three stages. In the first stage, collaboration is based on the interaction of peers, and includes six peer teaching efforts: the Science Mentor Program and also the Writing Fellows at Brown University, the Interdisciplinary General Education Program at California State Polytechnic University at Pomona, The Writing Center at Rhode Island College, the Community of Learners at Rollins College, and Urban Education at Westfield State College.

In the second stage, collaboration involves interaction of both faculty and students in both teaching and research. In stage three, collaboration addresses the interaction of students and faculty in curriculum design. Although stages two and three are not examples of peer teaching, faculty who are interested in the interaction of peers may wish to combine student collaboration with student-faculty collaboration.

Collaboration in educational settings means that both teachers and learners are active participants and this bridges the gulf between them. Collaboration creates a sense of community, and it means that knowledge is created, not transferred from teacher to student. Also, it locates knowledge in a community, rather than in the individual (Whipple 1987).

In an earlier report on student stress, a criticism made of student-faculty relationships was that, too often, students and faculty members did not seem to be connecting, and that such contacts were worth strengthening (Whitman, Spendlove, and Clark 1986).

Faculty-student interactions are valuable. Positive relationships with faculty, inside and outside the classroom, can help reduce student's stress and help them cope more effectively with stress. Faculty can play a key role in introducing and welcoming students to the academic community, beginning with the classroom as a microcosm of that community and extending outside the classroom as well (Whitman, Spendlove, and Clark 1986, p. 39).

What is striking about the experiences of faculty who have incorporated peer teaching efforts in their classrooms is the added contribution of building relationships between peer teachers and professors. Students feel honored to be asked to be peer teachers. They appreciate the training program conducted by their teachers. They enjoy the ongoing contact with faculty that peer teaching requires. In answering why students want to be peer teachers, Romer (1988) responded that, even where they are paid, that rarely is the reason. Rather, students like the chance to work with faculty and to get to know them better.

Summary
Providing students with opportunities to teach each other may be one of the most important educational services a teacher can render. Probably, what is best is a blending of professor-mediated and peer-mediated instruction. In other words, there are times when students need and want the presence of their professors, and times when they do not. Course directors can experiment with using previously successful students as teaching assistants and tutors to supplement large classes, as well as

with organizing students into work partners and groups to complete course requirements. In other words, there are times when students need and want to work alone and times when they prefer interaction with peers.

CONCLUSIONS AND RECOMMENDATIONS

Although we know that much human development takes place through the interaction of peers, the nature of these interactions is not well understood at the college level. While there is a considerable body of research in primary and secondary education suggesting that the student's commitment of time and energy to academic work is influenced strongly by peers, with potential for either positive or negative influence, similar relationships have not been studied as well at the college level (Astin 1985).

In particular, it would be helpful to know whether different peer groups can be used consciously to enhance the learner's commitment to academic work. The motivational, as well as cognitive, influence of peer groups should be addressed in the evaluation of peer teaching efforts; however, readers of the literature on peer teaching may conclude that there is a need for better studies. A minimum requirement for evaluating student tutoring programs, suggested by McKellar (1984) but found in few published reports, is to compare tutors and tutees with matched students who have had equal exposure to the learning matter. Similarly, the need for better evaluations of peer counseling programs was cited by Giddan and Austin (1982), who expressed concern that measurement of both short-term and long-term impact on recipients presented difficult problems. Specifically, they raised the problem of selecting control groups of sufficient similarity without withholding, or delaying, service to people of equal need for the sake of controlled research.

Most peer support programs are hampered by changes in organizational life: These programs *"don't stand still long enough to be measured"* (Giddan and Austin 1982, p. 182). This problem was acknowledged by a researcher who had hoped to set up a formal experiment to evaluate his peer program at San Jose State College. *"But in the process of working out an effective system, we were constantly making changes, and the practical difficulties made an experiment impossible"* (Finney 1975, p. 186).

Understandably, therefore, many published reports of peer program evaluations depend upon impressions. For example, Holzberg, Knapp, and Turner stated that their assessment of student volunteers at seven colleges was *"largely derived from anecdotal evidence"* (1966, p. 397). In their summary of the general methods of program evaluation, Anderson and Ball (1978, p. 65) counsel about the *"imprudence of prejudging and stereotyping 'hard' and 'soft' evaluations"*; nevertheless, they

It would be helpful to know whether different peer groups can be used consciously to enhance the learner's commitment to academic work.

conclude that most comprehensive program evaluations should include both components. The continuum of general methods of hard to soft includes experimental studies, quasiexperimental studies, correlation studies, surveys, participant assessments, systematic expert judgments, and case studies. In choosing the combination of methods that best suits their programs, the problem for program developers remains to find enough financial resources to do more than the minimum evaluation. Unfortunately, the resources needed to develop and implement an innovative program may preclude investing enough money to do more than the minimum program evaluation.

Although the research suggests that the effectiveness of peer teaching depends upon the types of training the student teachers received (Deming 1986), until better program evaluations are conducted, the evidence is not yet clear which is the best type of training. Also, it may be that not all students benefit equally from being taught by peers. Beach (1960) pre- and posttested students in an advanced educational psychology course at the University of Michigan. Students assigned to autonomous small groups that had no contact with an instructor, and who were above average on the S scale (social introversion-extroversion) of Guilford's Inventory of Factors, scored significantly higher in achievement gains than those who were below average. Conversely, less sociable students assigned to a traditional lecture format also made significant achievement gains. We do not know how generalizable to other groups the "sociability" factor is, and what other factors may influence the success or failure of peer-mediated instruction. The complexity of learning style preferences was highlighted in a recent report by Clayton and Murrell (1987).

A review of the literature also reveals a need to better study the role of the college professor in peer teaching. A researcher wondered whether, with the personal self-instruction use of a go-at-your-own-pace instructional package facilitated by student proctors, he was saying *"good-bye to teaching"* (Keller 1968, p. 79). Twenty years after the introduction of PSI, a question that remains unanswered is, When students do the teaching, how should we evaluate the college teacher? In the context of collaborative writing programs, a researcher indentified four features of the college teacher's performance that an evaluator should consider.

1. *The teacher should be evaluated as a **task-setter***. For ex-

ample, is there a good written statement of the student's writing assignment?

2. *The teacher should be evaluated as a* **classroom manager**. Does the teacher organize students into groups in an efficient manner?

3. *The teacher should be evaluated as a* **facilitator**. Does the teacher help groups progress, providing adequate assistance without interfering?

4. *The teacher should be evaluated as a* **synthesizer**. Does the teacher make sense out of student group work? (Wiener 1986).

In conclusion, the underlying principle for teacher evaluation is that

in the collaborative learning classroom, the instructor is in no sense a passive figure. Collaborative learning is not unstructured learning; it replaces one structure, the traditional one, with another, a collaborative structure (Wiener 1986, p. 61).

As the field of educational psychology shifts toward *cognitivism*—viewing the learner and his or her information processing strategies as the primary determiner of learning (Wittrock 1974)—the author hopes that educational researchers will include the student-as-teacher as a subject of study. Questions raised 15 years ago remain:

What characteristics make a good assistant? Do students know enough about (the subject) to teach? Should they be paid for their work? What is the effect on their peers? What is the effect on themselves? (Maas and Pressler 1973, p. 58).

Furthermore, there is a need to compare peer teachers to faculty teachers. In a literature review, a researcher found no studies describing a direct comparison between peer tutoring and tutoring by a teacher-expert under otherwise identical conditions (Cornwall 1979). In a critique of the gap between research and practice, Schön (1983) contends that researchers in the field of cognitive psychology have, in the past, offered little help to teachers. An educator, in agreement, pointed out that *"the questions driving research seem not to be the questions needed for practice, and efforts to connect the two have not been successful''* (Cross 1986, p. 13). In attempt to link research to practice, a Research Forum was established at the 1985 National Conference on Higher Education sponsored by the American Association of Higher Education. Its purpose is to involve educators in the creation of a research agenda that speaks to current educational concerns (Mentkowski and Chickering 1987). At the 1988 Research Forum, the following questions were generated by participants and shared later with researchers at the annual meeting of the American Educational Research Association:

1. How do students learn how to learn collaboratively?
2. What factors impede or contribute to students' abilities to increase their own learning to the maximum in a collaborative environment?
3. How does collaboration develop among learners with a wide disparity of knowledge and/or ability? How do we balance homogeneity and heterogeneity?
4. Are there individual differences in student characteristics, cognitive development, reasoning, and learning styles that interact with collaborative learning as a strategy? How does a collaborative environment affect, and interact with, these student differences? For example, does collaborative learning interfere with learning among dependent, or independent, learners?
5. If styles of learning lead to participation in collaborative projects, are there changes in the intellectual development cycle as a result of the participation, and are they different for different learning styles?
6. How does participation in collaborative projects influence career development?

An incisive review of student response groups in writing classrooms concluded that a number of questions remain unanswered about the nature of collaborative learning in general and peer teaching in particular. The review identified a need for more studies of the actual functioning of peer talk in the classroom, with descriptions of the classrooms themselves, and how classroom structures relate to peer structures. Research questions posed for interested investigators include the following:

How does peer talk about writing function in the writing classroom? How does peer talk fit the rest of the instruc-

tional agenda? When talking together, how do students give and receive response and support? (DiPardo and Freedman 1988, p. 143).

These research questions are relevant directly to co-peer teaching—partnerships and work groups. With little rewording, the same questions are relevant to near-peer teaching—teaching assistants, tutors, and counselors. It remains to be seen whether this mechanism facilitates research on peer teaching that will help educators plan and conduct effective programs. Certainly, the annual Research Forum has provided a large agenda, and the author hopes that educational researchers will view all the concerns expressed in this chapter as an *opportunity, not as criticism.*

Need for Evaluation

The fact that evaluation of peer teaching still is fairly primitive raises two points: (1) Faculty should proceed cautiously in starting new peer teaching programs, and (2) there is an enormous opportunity for evaluation studies. For example, a large area of needed research concerns the effects of cultural background on peer relations. Some students may come from a family or ethnic group in which decisions often are made by consensus; in other families or ethnic groups this is rare. Are students taught to question group members, or not to? To test students from diverse backgrounds for their ability to work in peer groups without taking into account familial and cultural differences may result in confusing findings.

How students deal with cultural diversity was addressed by a study group at Harvard and Radcliffe in the 1950s, where academic counselors were impressed by the range of student response to dormitory bull sessions—from a joyful sense of liberation to violent shock (Perry 1968). Current research would be welcome in identifying those most vulnerable to culture shock and most unable to benefit from peer influence. Also, it would be helpful to study methods of supporting and helping these students learn to learn from peers. Of course, a key cultural dimension concerns gender, and there is a growing body of research that addresses the higher education experience for women. It may suggest that relationships play a significant role in women's learning. Those interested in peer learning would be helped by research exploring the possible connections be-

tween peer teaching and women's learning (Belenky et al. 1986).

Recommendations from Current Literature
Despite those needs for additional research, seven recommendations are warranted by the current literature.

1. *Student peer groups are such a potent force in student development that, even if not always well understood, the curriculum should be organized to make use of them.* Without direction of the faculty, students influence each other anyway, probably in both positive and negative ways. With the direction of the faculty, the aim should be to channel this force in positive ways.

2. *Although, traditionally, students are expected to do their own work individually, learning also may occur when students work cooperatively.* When students eventually enter the work force, most will find that work requires both working alone and working with others. Peer teaching can help promote the skills of working with others, sharing one's strengths and supplementing weaknesses with the strengths of others.

3. *Both peer teachers and peer learners learn.* The benefits to both parties are cognitive and affective. In peer-mediated instruction, there is potential for students to learn a lot, and like what they learn.

4. *Involving students in the planning of peer teaching programs helps to develop future college teachers.* Most college teachers begin their apprenticeship as graduate teaching assistants. Peer teaching begins the process earlier and exposes students to less traditional methods of teaching.

5. *Students like to become peer teachers because they seek closer relationships with faculty.* Although it may be desirable to pay near-peers (student teaching assistants, tutors, and counselors), many students are motivated by the opportunity to get to know faculty. Peer teaching may promote mentor relationships that otherwise often do not begin until graduate or professional school training.

6. *Learning may increase with a blend of situations in which professors are present and are not present.* Certainly, with peer teaching, we are not saying "good-bye" to professors. Peer teaching provides an opportunity to increase

the resources available to students, not to substitute student teachers for faculty teachers.

7. *Allowing, or even contriving, situations in which students teach each other may be one of the most important services a teacher can render his, or her, students.* Faculty always have enjoyed the benefit of learning as a result of teaching. With peer teaching, we are extending these benefits to the student body.

The "Adultness" of Higher Education

As a final area of discussion, something must be said about the "adultness" of higher education and the contribution peer teaching can make to treating students as adults. In the 1960s, an educator introduced the term, *"andragogy"* (adult learning), and sought to establish a case for an important difference between the characteristics of adult learning and child learning (Knowles 1970). Prior to his influence, the term, *"pedagogy,"* was used to define the profession of teaching without any reference to age. Now, *"pedagogy"* is widely accepted as a term to refer to the teaching of children, and *"andragogy"* to the teaching of adults.

Peer teaching has roots in elementary education, including the one-room schoolroom in which older children supervised younger children. When and where peer teaching among children was successful, perhaps this was due to its treatment of children as adults. In other words, when given the opportunity to learn and study without direct adult supervision, many children respond in a responsible manner, that is, they act like adults. Ironically, when college students are subjected to an information-based (lecture), externally-rewarded (tests) educational system, perhaps we are treating them as children. Whether or not it is fair to call the negative behaviors of college students "childish," certainly the manifestations are all too familiar to faculty: cutting classes, sleeping in class, emphasis on grades ("Will it be on the test?"), and cheating.

Whether designing instruction for children or adults, a basic decision is made regarding who is responsible for making decisions for what is to be learned. Is it the teacher or the student? Teacher-centered instruction is the well-known model we have been exposed to since kindergarten. In the less familiar student-centered model, the teacher may provide the student with experience and guidance, but eventually, the student is expected to take responsibility for his, or her, own learning, identifying educational needs, the best manner for learning, and the pacing of learning (Barrows and Tamblyn 1980).

Advocates of peer-mediated instruction have used a type of peer teaching, student work groups, to promote student-centered instruction. They commented that students must learn what questions to ask, what questions not to ask, and when to ask:

> To learn in a meaningful way, they must teach themselves. The teacher can anticipate their problems, their questions, their concerns, but no teacher can learn for the student. . . . The teacher is not an intellectual surgeon, implanting a pacemaker in the student's brain, but rather a midwife who assists in the delivery of a free mind. (Wales and Stager 1978, p. viii).

Other educators have used the metaphor of the neurosurgeon and the midwife. A cognitive psychologist warned against assuming that you could walk into a classroom, unscrew the tops of students' skulls, peer intently into the brain of each student, and say something like, "Hmm, you seem to have this connection missing," and then proceed to add the necessary connections (Norman 1980). A teacher of religion and the humanities used the metaphor of Socrates that the instructor was a midwife to students pregnant with ideas. The educator recommended that teachers not directly convey what they know, but use what they know to convey to students what they themselves know or can know (Segal 1979).

Traditionally, education for children and adults is teacher-centered. Its advantage is that teachers can use their expertise to make sure that learners are exposed to the most important material. However, a disadvantage is that students may not learn to learn. In other words, they do not acquire the skill of determining what is worth learning. Since no teachers have signed a contract to teach students for the rest of their lives, the inability of students to guide their own learning can be a problem if a teacher's goal is to encourage lifelong learning.

Peer-mediated instruction is student-centered, at least for the peer teacher. Their involvement is active, and they feel responsible for learning the material—not to take a test, but to help another person. Of course, if peer teachers mimic the traditional methods of teaching, including the "I talk, you listen" mode of information delivery, then peer teaching will not be student-centered for the learners.

The final recommendation is that faculty and staff should resist using peers as substitute teachers. Instead, peer teachers should support fellow students in their efforts to learn. Since this report is not recommending the use of peers as substitute teachers, the challenge posed here is to devise ways of organizing peer teaching so that students are distanced as much as possible from identification as teacher surrogates. To some degree, peer groups always will be influenced by faculty. No peer relations within a college or university can ever be entirely autonomous. The issue to be resolved by readers of this report is how direct faculty should be in influencing peer relations in order to most tap peer influence.

REFERENCES

The Educational Resources Information Center (ERIC) Clearinghouse
on Higher Education abstracts and indexes the current literature on
higher education for inclusion in ERIC's data base and announcement
in ERIC's monthly bibliographic journal, *Resources in Education*
(RIE). Most of these publications are available through the ERIC
Document Reproduction Service (EDRS). For publications cited in this
bibliography that are available from EDRS, ordering number and price
are included. Readers who wish to order a publication should write to
the ERIC Document Reproduction Service, 3900 Wheeler Avenue,
Alexandria, Virginia 22304. (Phone orders with VISA or MasterCard
are taken at 800/227-ERIC or 703/823-0500). When ordering, please
specify the document (ED) number. Documents are available as noted
in microfiche (MF) and paper copy (PC). Because prices are subject to
change, it is advisable to check the latest issue of *Resources in
Education* for current cost based on the number of pages in the
publication.

Abercrombie, M.J.L. 1972. *The Anatomy of Judgment*. New York:
Basic Books.

Alexander, Laurence T., et al. 1974. "Peer-Assisted Learning."
Improving Human Performance Quarterly 3 (4): 175–86.

Allen, Amy R., and Boraks, Nancy. 1978. "Peer Tutoring: Putting It
to the Test." *Reading Teacher* 32 (3): 274–78.

Andersen, Margaret L. 1987. "Changing the Curriculum in Higher
Education." *Signs* 12 (2): 222–54.

Anderson, Scarvia B., and Ball, Samuel. 1978. *The Profession and
Practice of Program Evaluation*. San Francisco: Jossey-Bass.

Annis, Linda F. 1983. "The Processes and Effects of Peer Tutoring."
Montreal: Paper presented at The American Education Research
Association Annual Meeting. ED 228 964. 11 pp. MF–$1.07;
PC–$3.85.

Arbes, Bill H., and Kitchener, Karen G. 1974. "Faculty Consultation:
A Study in Support of Education through Student Interaction."
Journal of Counseling Psychology 21 (2): 121–26.

Astin, Alexander W. 1985. *Achieving Educational Excellence*. San
Francisco: Jossey-Bass.

———. 1987. "Competition or Cooperation." *Change* 19 (5): 12–19.

Bailey, Anne Lowery. 1986. "Faculty Leaders in Profile." *Change*
18 (4): 24–32, 37–47.

Bannister-Willis, Linda. 1984. "Developing a Peer Tutor Program."
In *Writing Centers: Theory and Administration*, edited by Gary A.
Olson. Urbana Ill.: National Council of Teachers of English.

Bargh, John A., and Schul, Yaakov. 1980. "On the Cognitive
Benefits of Teaching." *Journal of Educational Psychology* 72 (5):
593–604.

Barrows, Howard S., and Tamblyn, Robyn M. 1980. *Problem-Based Learning: An Approach to Medical Education.* New York: Springer Publishing Company.

Beach, Leslie R. 1960. "Sociability and Academic Achievement in Various Types of Learning Situations." *Journal of Educational Psychology* 51 (4): 208–12.

———. 1974. "Self-Directed Student Groups and College Learning." *Higher Education* 3 (2): 187–200.

Belenky, Mary F., Blythe M. Clinchy, Nancy R. Goldberger, and Jill M. Tarule. 1986. *Women's Ways of Knowing: The Development of Self, Voice and Mind.* New York: Basic Books.

Benesch, Sarah. 1985. "Metaresponse: A Hidden Benefit of Peer Writing Instruction." Houston: Paper presented at the National Council of Teachers of English Spring Conference. ED 262 413. 13 pp. MF–$1.07; PC–$3.85.

Benware, Carl A., and Deci, Edward L. 1984. "Quality of Learning with an Active Versus Passive Motivation Set." *American Educational Research Journal* 21 (4): 755–66.

Bouton, Clark, and Garth, Russell Y. 1983. "Conclusions and Resources." In *Learning in Groups*, edited by Clark Bouton and Russell Y. Garth. New Directions for Teaching and Learning No. 14, San Francisco: Jossey-Bass.

Bruffee, Kenneth. 1978. "The Brooklyn Plan: Attaining Intellectual Growth through Peer Influence." *Liberal Education* 54 (4): 447–68.

———. 1984. "Collaborative Learning and 'The Conversation of Mankind.'" *College English* 46 (6): 635–52.

———. 1986. "Social Construction, Language, and the Authority of Knowledge: A Bibliographical Essay." *College English* 48 (8): 773–90.

———. 1987. "The Art of Collaborative Learning." *Change* 19 (2): 42–47.

Cason, Carolyn L.; Cason, Gerald L.; and Bartnick, Dorothy A. 1977. "Peer Instruction in Professional Nurse Education: A Qualitative Study." *Journal of Nursing Education* 16 (7): 10–22.

Chickering, Arthur W., and Gamson, Zelda, F. 1987. "Seven Principles for Good Practice in Undergraduate Education." *AAHE Bulletin* 39 (7): 3–7. ED 282 491. 6pp. MF–$1.07; PC–$3.85.

Churchill, Ruth, and John, Paula. 1958. "Conservation of Teaching Time through the Use of Lecture Classes and Student Assistants." *Journal of Educational Psychology* 49 (6): 324–27.

Clayton, Charles S., and Murrell, Patricia H. 1987. *Learning Styles: Improving Educational Practices.* ASHE-ERIC Higher Education Report No. 4, Washington, D.C.: Association for the Study of Higher Education. ED 293 478. 116 pp. MF–$1.07; PC–$12.07.

Cobb, Loretta, and Elledge, Elaine Kivgore. 1984. "Undergraduate

Staffing in the Writing Center." In *Writing Center: Theory and Administration*, edited by Gary A. Olson. Urbana, Ill.: National Council of Teachers of English.

Coldeway, Dan O. 1980. "Exploring the Effects of Peer Tutoring in Distance Education." *Research and Evaluation of Distance Education for the Adult Learner*. Research Report No. 2. Edmonton, Alberta: Athabasca University. ED 258 224. 30 pp. MF–$1.07; PC–$5.79.

Coleman, Eve. 1987. "Response Groups as a Source of Data for Classroom Based Research." Paper presented at the Conference on College Composition and Communication Annual Meeting, Atlanta. ED 281 192. 19 pp. MF–$1.07; PC–$3.85.

Cornwall, Malcolm G. 1979. *Students as Teachers: Peer Teaching in Higher Education*. Amsterdam: University of Amsterdam.

Craig, Dorothy. 1978. *Hip Pocket Guide to Planning and Evaluation*. Austin, Tex.: Learning Concepts.

Cross, Patricia K. 1986. "A Proposal to Improve Teaching." *AAHE Bulletin* 39 (1): 9–15.

Davies, Norman F., and Omberg, Margaret. 1986. "Peer Group Teaching and the Composition Class." Paper read at the International Association of English as a Foreign Language Annual Meeting. Brighton, England. ED 274 159. 17 pp. MF–$1.07; PC–$3.85.

Davis, Robert. 1967. "Peer Group Teaching or Involving Students in Teaching." *Educational Development, Report No. 14*. East Lansing: Michigan State University.

DeCiccio, Albert C., et al. 1986. "Merrimack College Peer Tutor Training Tape." North Andover, Mass: Merrimack College. ED 283 143. 16 pp. MF–$1.07; PC–$3.85.

Deming, Mary P. 1986. "Peer Tutoring and the Teaching of Writing." Paper presented at the Southeastern Writing Center Association April Meeting, Mobile, Ala. ED 276 019. 27 pp. MF–$1.07; PC–$5.79.

deSilva, Deema, and Freund, Elizabeth. 1985. "A Tutor Handbook for a TRIO Programs: Operation Success." Wichita, Kans.: Wichita State University. ED 269 492. 83 pp. MF–$1.07; PC–$10.13.

Diamond, Michael J. 1972. "Improving the Undergraduate Lecture Class by Use of Student-Led Discussion Groups." *American Psychologist* 27 (10): 978–81.

Di Pardo, Anne, and Freedman, Sarah Warshauer. 1988 "Peer Response Groups in the Writing Classroom: Theoretic Foundations and New Directions." *Review of Educational Research* 58 (2): 119–49.

Dugger, Ronnie. 1978. "Collaborative Learning: Changing the Power Relationships." In *Guide to Effective Teaching*, editors of *Change*. New Rochelle, N.Y.: Change Magazine Press.

Durling, Rich, and Schick, Connie. 1976. "Concept Attainment by Pairs and Individuals as a Function of Vocalization." *Journal of Educational Psychology* 68 (1): 83–91.

Egerton, John. 1978. "Teaching Learning While Learning to Teach." In *Guide to Effective Teaching*, editors of *Change*. New Rochelle, N.Y.: Change Magazine Press.

Ehly, Stewart, and Eliason, Michele. 1980. "Peer Tutoring: References from the Education and Psychology Literature." Iowa City: The University of Iowa. ED 198 077. 37 pp. MF–$1.07; PC–$5.79.

————, and Larsen, Stephen C. 1980. *Peer Tutoring for Individualized Instruction*. Boston: Allyn and Bacon, Inc.

Ellner, Carolyn L., and Barnes, Carol P. 1983. *Studies of College Teaching*. Lexington, Mass.: D.C. Heath and Company.

Ferrier, Barbara; Marrin, Michael; and Seigman, Jeffrey. 1988. "Student Autonomy in Learning Medicine: Some Participants' Experiences." In *Developing Student Autonomy in Learning*. 2nd ed, edited by David Boud. New York: Nichols Publishing Company.

Finney, Ben C. 1975. "The Peer Program: An Experiment in Humanistic Education." In *Psychological Stress in the Campus Community*, edited by B. Bloom. New York: Behavioral Publications.

Fuhrmann, Barbara Schneider, and Grasha, Anthony F. 1983. *A Practical Handbook for College Teachers*. Boston: Little, Brown and Company.

Gartner, Alan; Kohler, Mary; and Riessmann, Frank. 1971. *Children Teach Children: Learning by Teaching*. New York: Harper and Row.

Gebhardt, Richard. 1980. "Teamwork and Feedback: Broadening the Base of Collaborative Writing." *College English* 42 (1): 69–73.

Gere, Anne Ruggles. 1987. *Writing Groups: History, Theory, and Implications*. Carbondale: Southern Illinois University Press.

Giddan, Norman S., and Austin, M.J., editors. 1982. *Peer Counseling and Self-Help Groups on Campus*. Springfield, Ill.: Charles C. Thomas.

Glassman, Susan. 1984. "Training Peer Tutors Using Video." Paper presented at the Conference on College Composition and Communication Annual Meeting, New York City. ED 252 875. 12 pp. MF–$1.07; PC–$3.85.

Goldschmid, Barbara, and Goldschmid, Marcel L. 1976. "Peer Teaching in Higher Education: A Review." *Higher Education* 5 (1): 9–33.

Goldschmid, Marcel L. 1970. "Instructional Options: Adapting the Large University Course to Individual Differences." *Learning and Development* 1 (5): 1–2.

————. 1971. "The Learning Cell: An Instructional Innovation." *Learning and Development* 2 (5): 1–6.

————. 1976. "Teaching and Learning in Higher Education: Recent Trends." *Higher Education* 5 (4): 437–56.

Grasha, Anthony F. 1972. "Observations of Relating Teaching Goals to Student Response Styles and Classroom Methods." *American Psychologist* 27 (2): 144–47.

Hardaway, Francine. 1975. "What Students Can Do to Take the Burden Off You." *College English* 36 (5): 577–79.

Harrington, Judy, and Moore, Diane. 1986. "Saying 'Si' to Supplementals." Paper presented at the Rocky Mountain Regional Conference of the International Reading Association Annual Meeting, Colorado Springs. ED 270 739. 17 pp. MF–$1.07; PC–$3.85.

Harris, Jeanette. 1984. "The Handbook as a Supplement to a Tutor Training Program." In *Writing Centers: Theory and Administration*, edited by Gary A. Olson. Urbana, Ill: National Council of Teachers of English.

Hawkins, Thom. 1980. "Intimacy and Audience: The Relationship between Revision and the Social Dimension of Peer Teaching." *College English* 42 (1): 64–68.

Hendelman, Walter J., and Boss, Marvin. 1986. "Reciprocal Peer Teaching by Medical Students in the Gross Anatomy Laboratory." *Journal of Medical Education* 61 (8): 674–80.

Heywood, Peter. 1988. "The Science Mentor Program in Undergraduate Science Courses." *Journal of College Science Teaching* 17(14): 212–14, 245.

Highet, George. 1950. *The Art of Teaching*. New York: Knopf.

Holt, Mara Dawn. 1988. "Collaborative Learning from 1911–1986: A Sociohistorical Analysis." Ph.D. dissertation, University of Texas, Austin.

Holzberg, Jules D.; Knapp, Robert; and Turner, John L. 1966. "Companionship with the Mentally Ill: Effects on the Personalities of College Student Volunteers." *Psychiatry* 29 (4): 395–405.

Hvitfeldt, Christina. 1986. "Guided Peer Critique in ESL Writing at the College Level." Paper presented at the Japan Association of Language Teaching and Learning, Annual Meeting, Hammamatsu, Japan. ED 282 438. 11 pp. MF–$1.07; PC–$3.85.

Jacques, David. 1984. *Learning in Groups*. Dover, N.H.: Croon Helm.

Janssen, Peter. 1978. "Undergraduate TAs: Motivated and Well-Prepared." In *Guide to Effective Teaching*, editors of *Change*. New Rochelle, N.Y.: Change Magazine Press.

Keller, Fred. 1968. "Goodbye Teacher. . ." *Journal of Applied Behavior Analysis* 1 (1): 79–89.

————. 1974. "Ten Years of Personalized Instruction." *Teaching of Psychology* 1 (1): 4–9.

Kitchener, Karen G., and Hurst, James C. 1972. *Education through Student Interaction Manual*. Fort Collins: Colorado State University.

Knowles, Malcolm. 1970. *The Modern Practice of Adult Education*. New York: Association Press.

Knox, Alan B. 1980. "Helping Teachers Help Adults Learn." In *Teaching Adults Effectively*, edited by Alan B. Knox. New Directions for Continuing Education No. 6, San Francisco: Jossey-Bass.

Lincoln, C. Eric. 1978. "Students as Facilitators." In *Guide to Effective Teaching*, editors of *Change*. New Rochelle, N.Y.: Change Magazine Press.

Lippitt, Peggy, and Lippitt, Ronald. 1968. "Cross-age Helpers." *NEA Journal* 57 (March): 4.

Maas, James B., and Pressler, Virginia M. 1973. "When Students Become Teachers." *Behavioral and Social Science Teacher* 1 (1): 55–60.

Martin, Warren Bryan. 1981. "Introduction." In *New Perspectives in Teaching and Learning*, edited by Warren Bryan Martin. New Directions for Teaching and Learning No. 7, San Francisco: Jossey-Bass.

Mayhew, Lewis B., and Ford, Patrick J. 1971. *Changing the Curriculum*. San Francisco: Jossey-Bass.

McKellar, Nancy A. 1984. "Peer Tutoring: An Evaluation of the Relative Cognitive Benefits." Paper presented at the National Association of School Psychologists Convention, Philadelphia. ED 258 933. 14 pp. MF–$1.07; PC–$3.85.

Meeth, L. Richard. 1978. "Introduction: Peer Teaching," and "The Participatory Classroom." In *Guide to Effective Teaching*, editors of *Change*. New Rochelle, N.Y.: Change Magazine Press.

Mentkowski, Marcia, and Chickering, Arthur W. 1987. "Linking Educators and Researchers in Setting a Research Agenda for Undergraduate Education." *The Review of Higher Education* 11(2): 137–60.

Michaelsen, Larry K. 1983. "Team Learning in Large Classes." In *Learning in Groups*, edited by Clark Bouton and Russell Y. Garth. New Directions for Teaching and Learning No. 14, San Francisco: Jossey-Bass.

Moffett, James. 1968. *Teaching the Universe of Discourse*. Boston: Houghton-Mifflin.

Mood, Alexander M. 1970. "Do Teachers Make A Difference?" In *Do Teachers Make a Difference: A Report on Recent Research on Pupil Achievement*. Washington, D.C.: U.S. Office of Education.

Moore, David, and Poppino, Mary. 1983. *Successful Tutoring: A Practical Guide to Adult Learning Processes*. Springfield, Ill.: Charles C. Thomas.

Newcomb, Theodore. 1962. "Student Peer Group Influence." In *The American College*, edited by Nevitt Sanford. New York: John Wiley and Sons.

Norman, Donald. 1980. "What Goes on in the Mind of the Learner." In *Learning, Cognition, and College Teaching*, edited by Wilbert J. McKeachie. New Directions for Teaching and Learning No. 2, San Francisco: Jossey-Bass.

Olson, Gary A., editor. 1984. *Writing Centers: Theory and Administration*. Urbana, Ill.: National Council of Teachers of English.

Palmer, Parker. 1987. "Community, Conflict, and Ways of Knowing." *Change* 19 (5): 20–25.

Pepe, Evelyn A.: Hodel, Christine G.; and Bosshart, Donald A. 1980. "The Use of Peers to Teach Interviewing and Clinical Problem Solving." *Journal of Medical Education* 55 (9): 800.

Perry, William G. 1968. *Forms of Intellectual and Ethical Development: A Scheme*. New York: Holt, Rinehart and Winston, Inc.

Pierce, Mary McNeil; Stahlbrand, Kristina; and Armstrong, Suzanne Bryant. 1984. *Increasing Student Productivity through Peer Tutoring Programs*. Austin, Tex.: Pro-Ed.

Raimi, Ralph A. April 26, 1981. "Twice Told Tale: The Joy of Teaching." *The New York Times Spring Survey of Education*: 58–59.

Rasool, Joan, and Tatum, Travis. 1988. "Influencing Student Reality and Academic Performance." Paper read at the 1988 Freshman Year Experience Conference, East Columbia, South Carolina. Author.

Riessman, Frank. 1965. "The 'Helper-Therapy' Principle." *Social Work* 10 (2): 27–32.

Riley, Roberta D., and Huffman, Gail M. 1980. "Peer Support during Student Teaching: A Shared Partnership." Ed 194 468. 13 pp. MF–$1.07; PC–$3.85.

Rizzolo, Patricia. 1982. "Peer Tutors Make Good Teachers." *Improving College and University Teaching* 30 (3): 115–19.

Romer, Karen T. 1985. *Models of Collaboration in Undergraduate Education*. Providence, R.I.: Brown University. Pamphlet.

———. 1988. "Can Undergraduates Serve in the Classroom?" *George Street Journal* 12 (10): 8.

Roon, Robert J., et al. 1983. "The Experimental Use of Cooperative Learning Groups in a Biochemistry Laboratory Course for First Year Medical Students." *Biochemical Education* 11 (1): 1–5.

Schon, Donald. 1983. *The Reflective Practitioner*. New York: Basic Books.

Schunk, Dale H. 1987. "Peer Models and Children's Behavioral Change." *Review of Educational Research* 57 (2): 149–74.

Schwenk, Thomas L., and Whitman, Neal. 1984. *Residents as Teachers*. Salt Lake City: University of Utah School of Medicine.

———. 1987. *Physicians as Teachers*. Baltimore: Williams and Wilkins.

Segal, Robert. September 24, 1979. "What is Good Teaching and Why Is There So Little of It?" *The Chronicle of Higher Education* 19 (4): 21.

Slotnick, Robert S.; Jeger, Abraham M.; and Schure, Matthew. 1981. "Peer Support Networks in a Large Introductory Psychology Class." Paper presented at American Psychological Association National Convention, Los Angeles. ED 209 629. 8 pp. MF–$1.07; PC–$3.85.

Starks, Gretchen. 1984. "A Successful Peer Tutor Program to Improve Retention." Canandaigua, N.Y.: Community College of the Finger Lakes. ED 263 938. 23 pp. MF–$1.07; PC–$3.85.

Sugnet, Charles J. 1978. "The Power of a Supportive Environment." In *Guide to Effective Teaching*, editors of *Change*. New Rochelle, N.Y.: Change Magazine Press.

Taylor, Harold. 1969. *Students without Teachers: The Crisis in the University*. New York: Avon Books.

Thomas, Ellen S. 1982. "Final Report of Project C.O.P.S. Phase I. 1981–1982." Edison, N.J.: Middlesex County College. ED 230 781. 92 pp. MF–$1.07; PC–$10.13.

Tighe, M.J. 1971. "Creative Dialogue: Teaching Students to Teach Themselves." *New Directions in Teaching* 2 (4): 21–25.

Trevino, Fernando M., and Eiland, Jr., D.C. 1980. "Evaluation of a Basic Science Peer Tutorial Program for First- and Second-Year Medical Students." *Journal of Medical Education* 55 (11): 952–53.

Tyler, Ralph W. 1975. "Wasting Time and Resources in Schools and Colleges." *Viewpoints* 51 (March): 69.

Vattano, Frank S., et al. 1973. "Employing Undergraduate Students in the Teaching of Psychology. *Teaching of Psychology Newsletter* (March): 9–12.

Wagner, Jon. 1987. "Teaching and Research as Student Responsibilities." *Change* 19 (5): 26–35.

Wagner, Lilya. 1982. *Peer Teaching: Historical Perspectives*. Westport, Conn.: Greenwood Press.

Wales, Charles A., and Stager, Robert A. 1978. *The Guided Design Approach*. Englewood Cliffs, N.J.: Educational Technology Publications.

Walker, Carolyn; Von Bargen, Patrick; and Wessner, Dan. 1980. "Academic Tutoring at the Learning Assistance Center." Paper presented at the Western College Reading Association Annual

Meeting, San Francisco. ED 186 871. 17 pp. MF–$1.07;
PC–$3.85.

Walker-Bartnick, Leslie A.; Berger, John H.; and Kappelman, Murray
M. 1984. "A Model for Peer Tutoring in the Medical School
Setting." *Journal of Medical Education* 59 (4): 309–15.

Webb, Noreen M. 1982. "Student Interaction and Learning in Small
Groups." *Review of Educational Research* 52 (3): 421–45.

Whipple, William R. 1987. "Collaborative Learning: Recognizing It
When We See It." *AAHE Bulletin* 40 (2): 3–7.

Whitman, Neal; Spendlove, David C.; and Clark, Claire. 1984.
Student Stress: Effects and Solutions. ASHE-ERIC Higher
Education Report No. 2, Washington, D.C.: Association for the
Study of Higher Education. ED 246 832. 115 pp. MF–$1.07;
PC–$12.07.

———. 1986. *Increasing Students' Learning: A Faculty Guide to
Reducing Stress among Students*. ASHE-ERIC Higher Education
Report No. 4, Washington, D.C.: Association for the Study of
Higher Education. ED 274 264. 101 pp. MF–$1.07; PC–$12.07.

Wiener, Harvey S. 1986. "Collaborative Learning in the Classroom:
A Guide to Evaluation." *College English* 48 (1): 52–61.

Williams, Richard W. 1981. "Developing a Peer Tutoring Program: A
Self-Instructional Module." Chicago: Malcolm X College. ED 207
632. 55 pp. MF–$1.07; PC–$7.73.

Wittrock, Merlin C. 1974. "Learning as a Generative Process."
Educational Psychologist 11 (2): 87–95.

Wrigley, Charles. 1973. "Undergraduate Students as Teachers:
Apprenticeship in the University Classroom." *Teaching of
Psychology Newsletter* (March): 5–7.

Zander, Alvin. 1962. "Resistance to Change: Its Analysis and
Prevention." In *The Planning of Change*, edited by Warren Bennis,
Kenneth Benne, and Robert Chin. New York: Holt, Rinehart, and
Winston.

INDEX

A

Academic achievement
      success predictor, 37
      two-year gains, 4
Academic Improvement Center (Metropolitan State College), 40
Academically underprepared, 21, 22, 40
Action Committee on Collaborative Learning (AAHE), 4
Active learning, 4
Administrative factors, 34–35
"Adultness" of higher education, 61
Advertising, 35
Affective benefits, 7–8
Alcoholics Anonymous, 7
American Association of Higher Education, 4, 10, 58
American Educational Research Association, 58
Andragogy, 61
Antioch College, 15
Archons, 2
Aristotle, 2
Athabasca University (Canada), 33
Attrition reduction, 21
Authority: nature of, 11
Avoidance response style, 46

B

Bales' Observation System, 47
Benefits
      academic gains, 4, 20
      affective, 7–8
      attrition reduction, 21
      cognitive, 5–7
      emotional support, 25–26
      social goals, 30
      teacher/learner, 18, 49, 60–61
      teacher time saving, 14, 15, 28
      writing programs, 23
Block scheduling, 4
Boston University, 4
Brooklyn College, 23, 36, 38, 50
"Brooklyn Plan" (see Brooklyn College)
Brown University
      faculty skepticism, 33

ASHE-ERIC HIGHER EDUCATION REPORTS

Since 1983, the Association for the Study of Higher Education (ASHE) and the ERIC Clearinghouse on Higher Education, a sponsored project of the School of Education and Human Development at the George Washington University, have cosponsored the ASHE-ERIC Higher Education Report series. The 1988 series is the seventeenth overall, with the American Association for Higher Education having served as cosponsor before 1983.

Each monograph is the definitive analysis of a tough higher education problem, based on thorough research of pertinent literature and institutional experiences. After topics are identified by a national survey, noted practitioners and scholars write the reports, with experts reviewing each manuscript before publication.

Eight monographs (10 monographs before 1985) in the ASHE-ERIC Higher Education Report series are published each year, available individually or by subscription. Subscription to eight issues is $60 regular; $50 for members of AERA, AAHE, and AIR; $40 for members of ASHE (add $10.00 for postage outside the United States).

Prices for single copies, including 4th class postage and handling, are $15.00 regular and $11.25 for members of AERA, AAHE, AIR, and ASHE ($10.00 regular and $7.50 for members for 1985 to 1987 reports, $7.50 regular and $6.00 for members for 1983 and 1984 reports, $6.50 regular and $5.00 for members for reports published before 1983). If faster postage is desired for U.S. and Canadian orders, add $1.00 for each publication ordered; overseas, add $5.00. For VISA and MasterCard payments, include card number, expiration date, and signature. Orders under $25 must be prepaid. Bulk discounts are available on orders of 15 or more reports (not applicable to subscriptions). Order from the Publications Department, ASHE-ERIC Higher Education Reports, The George Washington University, One Dupont Circle, Suite 630, Washington, D.C. 20036-1183, or phone us at 202/296-2597. Write for a publications list of all the Higher Education Reports available.

1988 ASHE-ERIC Higher Education Reports

1. The Invisible Tapestry: Culture in American Colleges and Universities
   George D. Kuh and Elizabeth J. Whitt

2. Critical Thinking: Theory, Research, Practice, and Possibilities
   Joanne Gainen Kurfiss

3. Developing Academic Programs: The Climate for Innovation
   Daniel T. Seymour

4. Peer Teaching: To Teach is To Learn Twice
   Neal A. Whitman

1987 ASHE-ERIC Higher Education Reports

1. Incentive Early Retirement Programs for Faculty: Innovative Responses to a Changing Environment
   Jay L. Chronister and Thomas R. Kepple, Jr.

2. Working Effectively with Trustees: Building Cooperative Campus Leadership
   Barbara E. Taylor

3. Formal Recognition of Employer-Sponsored Instruction: Conflict and

Collegiality in Postsecondary Education
Nancy S. Nash and Elizabeth M. Hawthorne

4. Learning Styles: Implications for Improving Educational Practices
Charles S. Claxton and Patricia H. Murrell

5. Higher Education Leadership: Enhancing Skills through Professional Development Programs
Sharon A. McDade

6. Higher Education and the Public Trust: Improving Stature in Colleges and Universities
Richard L. Alfred and Julie Weissman

7. College Student Outcomes Assessment: A Talent Development Perspective
Maryann Jacobi, Alexander Astin, and Frank Ayala, Jr.

8. Opportunity from Strength: Strategic Planning Clarified with Case Examples
Robert G. Cope

1986 ASHE-ERIC Higher Education Reports

1. Post-tenure Faculty Evaluation: Threat or Opportunity?
Christine M. Licata

2. Blue Ribbon Commissions and Higher Education: Changing Academe from the Outside
Janet R. Johnson and Lawrence R. Marcus

3. Responsive Professional Education: Balancing Outcomes and Opportunities
Joan S. Stark, Malcolm A. Lowther, and Bonnie M.K. Hagerty

4. Increasing Students' Learning: A Faculty Guide to Reducing Stress among Students
Neal A. Whitman, David C. Spendlove, and Claire H. Clark

5. Student Financial Aid and Women: Equity Dilemma?
Mary Moran

6. The Master's Degree: Tradition, Diversity, Innovation
Judith S. Glazer

7. The College, the Constitution, and the Consumer Student: Implications for Policy and Practice
Robert M. Hendrickson and Annette Gibbs

8. Selecting College and University Personnel: The Quest and the Questions
Richard A. Kaplowitz

1985 ASHE-ERIC Higher Education Reports

1. Flexibility in Academic Staffing: Effective Policies and Practices
Kenneth P. Mortimer, Marque Bagshaw, and Andrew T. Masland

2. Associations in Action: The Washington, D.C., Higher Education Community
Harland G. Bloland

3. And on the Seventh Day: Faculty Consulting and Supplemental Income
Carol M. Boyer and Darrell R. Lewis

4. Faculty Research Performance: Lessons from the Sciences and Social Sciences
   John W. Creswell

5. Academic Program Reviews: Institutional Approaches, Expectations, and Controversies
   Clifton F. Conrad and Richard F. Wilson

6. Students in Urban Settings: Achieving the Baccalaureate Degree
   Richard C. Richardson, Jr., and Louis W. Bender

7. Serving More Than Students: A Critical Need for College Student Personnel Services
   Peter H. Garland

8. Faculty Participation in Decision Making: Necessity or Luxury?
   Carol E. Floyd

1984 ASHE-ERIC Higher Education Reports

1. Adult Learning: State Policies and Institutional Practices
   K. Patricia Cross and Anne-Marie McCartan

2. Student Stress: Effects and Solutions
   Neal A. Whitman, David C. Spendlove, and Claire H. Clark

3. Part-time Faculty: Higher Education at a Crossroads
   Judith M. Gappa

4. Sex Discrimination Law in Higher Education: The Lessons of the Past Decade
   J. Ralph Lindgren, Patti T. Ota, Perry A. Zirkel, and Nan Van Gieson

5. Faculty Freedoms and Institutional Accountability: Interactions and Conflicts
   Steven G. Olswang and Barbara A. Lee

6. The High-Technology Connection: Academic/Industrial Cooperation for Economic Growth
   Lynn G. Johnson

7. Employee Educational Programs: Implications for Industry and Higher Education
   Suzanne W. Morse

8. Academic Libraries: The Changing Knowledge Centers of Colleges and Universities
   Barbara B. Moran

9. Futures Research and the Strategic Planning Process: Implications for Higher Education
   James L. Morrison, William L. Renfro, and Wayne I. Boucher

10. Faculty Workload: Research, Theory, and Interpretation
    Harold E. Yuker

1983 ASHE-ERIC Higher Education Reports

1. The Path to Excellence: Quality Assurance in Higher Education
   Laurence R. Marcus, Anita O. Leone, and Edward D. Goldberg

2. Faculty Recruitment, Retention, and Fair Employment: Obligations and

Opportunities
John S. Waggaman

3. Meeting the Challenges: Developing Faculty Careers*
Michael C.T. Brookes and Katherine L. German

4. Raising Academic Standards: A Guide to Learning Improvement
Ruth Talbott Keimig

5. Serving Learners at a Distance: A Guide to Program Practices
Charles E. Feasley

6. Competence, Admissions, and Articulation: Returning to the Basics in Higher Education
Jean L. Preer

7. Public Service in Higher Education: Practices and Priorities
Patricia H. Crosson

8. Academic Employment and Retrenchment: Judicial Review and Administrative Action
Robert M. Hendrickson and Barbara A. Lee

9. Burnout: The New Academic Disease*
Winifred Albizu Meléndez and Rafael M. de Guzmán

10. Academic Workplace: New Demands, Heightened Tensions
Ann E. Austin and Zelda F. Gamson

*Out-of-print. Available through EDRS.

Order Form

QUANTITY   AMOUNT

_____ Please enter my subscription to the 1988 ASHE-ERIC
Higher Education Reports at $60.00, 50% off the cover
price, beginning with Report 1, 1988.   _____

_____ Please enter my subscription to the 1989 ASHE-ERIC
Higher Education Reports at $80.00, 33% off the cover
price, beginning with Report 1, 1989.   _____

_____ Outside U.S., add $10.00 per series for postage.   _____

Individual reports are available at the following prices:
1988 and forward, $15.00 per copy.   1983 and 1984, $7.50 per copy.
1985 to 1987, $10.00 per copy.   1982 and back, $6.50 per copy.

Book rate postage, U.S. only, is included in the price.
For fast U.P.S. shipping within the U.S., add $1.00 per book.
Outside U.S., please add $1.00 per book for surface shipping.
For air mail service outside U.S., add $5.00 per book.
All orders under $25 must be prepaid.

PLEASE SEND ME THE FOLLOWING REPORTS:

QUANTITY   TITLE   AMOUNT
_____ Report NO. ____ (_____)   _____
_____ Report NO. ____ (_____)   _____
_____ Report NO. ____ (_____)   _____
                                   SUBTOTAL: _____
                                   POSTAGE (see above) _____
                                   TOTAL AMOUNT DUE: _____

Please check one of the following:

☐ Check enclosed, payable to ASHE.
☐ Purchase order attached.
☐ Charge my credit card indicated below:
                 ☐ VISA   ☐ MasterCard

Expiration date _____

Name _____

Title _____

Institution _____

Address _____

City _____ State _____ Zip _____

Phone _____ Signature _____

ALL ORDERS SHOULD BE SENT TO:
ASHE-ERIC Higher Education Reports
The George Washington University
One Dupont Circle, Suite 630, Dept. RC
Washington, DC 20036-1183
Phone: 202/296-2597